AUTHENTICALLY
Alive

Soaring Within
Christ's Love-Light

Lois,
What a beautiful woman of faith and inspiration you are to me! You radiant the love of Christ. Shine On,
Nancy

NANCY ANN GARDNER

WestBow Press
A DIVISION OF THOMAS NELSON
& ZONDERVAN

Copyright © 2018 Nancy Ann Gardner.

All rights reserved. No part of this book may be used or reproduced by any means, graphic, electronic, or mechanical, including photocopying, recording, taping or by any information storage retrieval system without the written permission of the author except in the case of brief quotations embodied in critical articles and reviews.

This book is a work of non-fiction. Unless otherwise noted, the author and the publisher make no explicit guarantees as to the accuracy of the information contained in this book and in some cases, names of people and places have been altered to protect their privacy.

WestBow Press books may be ordered through booksellers or by contacting:

WestBow Press
A Division of Thomas Nelson & Zondervan
1663 Liberty Drive
Bloomington, IN 47403
www.westbowpress.com
1 (866) 928-1240

Because of the dynamic nature of the Internet, any web addresses or links contained in this book may have changed since publication and may no longer be valid. The views expressed in this work are solely those of the author and do not necessarily reflect the views of the publisher, and the publisher hereby disclaims any responsibility for them.

Any people depicted in stock imagery provided by Getty Images are models, and such images are being used for illustrative purposes only. Certain stock imagery © Getty Images.

ISBN: 978-1-9736-2946-7 (sc)
ISBN: 978-1-9736-2948-1 (hc)
ISBN: 978-1-9736-2947-4 (e)

Library of Congress Control Number: 2018906381

Print information available on the last page.

WestBow Press rev. date: 7/27/2018

Scripture quotations marked MSG are taken from THE MESSAGE, copyright © 1993, 1994, 1995, 1996, 2000, 2001, 2002 by Eugene H. Peterson. Used by permission of NavPress. All rights reserved. Represented by Tyndale House Publishers, Inc.

Scripture quotations marked (NIV) are taken from the Holy Bible, New International Version®, NIV®. Copyright © 1973, 1978, 1984, 2011 by Biblica, Inc.™ Used by permission of Zondervan. All rights reserved worldwide. www.zondervan.com The "NIV" and "New International Version" are trademarks registered in the United States Patent and Trademark Office by Biblica, Inc.

Scripture quotations marked (NLT) are taken from the Holy Bible, New Living Translation, copyright ©1996, 2004, 2015 by Tyndale House Foundation. Used by permission of Tyndale House Publishers, Inc., Carol Stream, Illinois 60188. All rights reserved.

Scripture quotations marked (TLB) are taken from The Living Bible copyright © 1971. Used by permission of Tyndale House Publishers, Inc.

Contents

Authentically ALIVE xi
Foreword xiii
The Wondrous Weaver xiii
Author's Note xvii

Section I: An Overview of the Winged Journey

Spiritual Sightings xxi

Chapter 1: God's Most Meaningful Metamorphosis

I Stand 5
Why, Oh Why? The Analogy of the Butterfly 7
The Soul's Sweet Spot 11
Perfect Suit of Wings 13
Crooked Halos and Broken Wings 15
Wake Up, O Sleeper 19
Suffocating in Self-Denial 23
The Dawn of a New Day 27
Made for More 29
On the Wing of a Prayer 33
Soul Surrender 37
Pay Close Attention 41
Just Be 47
Boundaryless Brooks and Empty Wells 53
Garlanded in Grace 59
Traveling Upward and Onward 63

Section II : The Inner Line to the Transformative Touch

Chapter 2 : Covered and Attempting Flight

Graceless and Grounded 73
Fig-Leaf Garments 79
Storied 85
Crippling Caterpillar Syndrome 91
The Master Locksmith 95
Sowing My Soul 99

Chapter 3 : Choosing to Uncover

Uncomfortably Clenched 105
The Holy Holder 109
Anchored in the Almighty 111
Worthless Wardrobe 115

Chapter 4 : Sacred Stillness

The God Who Sees 137
His Reflection Mirrored Back 141
An Uncontrollable Spin 147

Chapter 5 : The Chrysalis of Christ

The Art of Cocooning 159

Chapter 6 : Growing Wings

Wild and Cageless 171
The Butterfly Effect 175
Reintroduction 181
Feeding the Right Wolf 185

Chapter 7 : Transformed and Taking Flight

Beyond the Blue Yonder 195
A Kingly Kindness through Ki 199

Chapter 8 : Soaring within Christ's Love-Light

Acknowledgments 217
About the Author 219
Significance of Sculpture 221

Authentically ALIVE

In dedication to the mightiest of Monarchs, my mother Vivian Agnes Mehlhoff. My beloved Mom gave me not only my biological birth, but my spiritual one as well. Her self-sacrificing devotion of love, prayer, and belief honors her as the founder to the finding of my wings. Mom believed in my flight before I could even crawl. She never gave up on the knowing of my wings. Although today she soars higher still in the heavenlies, she is ever close within. I love you, Mom. Thank you for giving to the Lord. I have a life that's been changed.

And honorably, Dad, you get the first copy. Happy 90th Birthday! You continue to be an exceptional example of inspiration to me and mine. You are the fierce finisher in our family. I love you with the whole of my heart.

Welcome Readers,

I already consider YOU a friend. And I don't take your friendship lightly. I've prayed for God to hold our time together in His holy care. We are sojourners embarking on our spiritual journeys together. I want to thank you for choosing to pick up this book. Through this action alone, you are claiming Spirit-filled growth in your life. And although I hold hopes for a more unlimited target-reading audience, I do have a passionate ache for the church-pew attendee. Let us fiercely battle together for chainlessness. We are sealed to arise to our individual freedom flights. May we find ourselves courageously fighting for such ordained liberty!

I truly never dreamt I'd write a book. It has often felt at times as though I'm wearing a bikini (much beyond the appropriate age) in public view and revealing my cellulite and spider veins for all eyes to see. I know the ramifications can be harsh. So, as you read on, may you be graced with sight to see the Living God over any fragilities through my written words. I am grateful that I no longer let this be of any concern of mine. Such thoughts stem from pebbles of pride. His Spirit nudgings remained ruthless, and I knew the writing was a way of expressing His heart-song back. May this book inspire your faith wings to fly even farther on, within your own unique, intimate spiritual journey. My prayer is that through the writings, you will find similar parallels, insightful junctions, and personal touches that will speak and put a spark into your personal soul travel. May this become a voyage of deeper intimacy with God, as you encounter your more authentic, real self. You are adventuring with the truest of all relationships, our most beloved comrade, Jesus Christ. He aches to grace in full abundance. You are beyond precious in His sight and mine too.

Foreword

The Wondrous Weaver

Father God,

 Thank you, Lord, for every thread in the tapestry of my life. The dark threads, as well as the threads of gold. Your wondrous weaving, stitch by loving stitch, has brought me to this very place. A place that is embarking on yet another new season with You. Another sacred season but with a different purpose of Yours in mind. This time, not in an entirety for personal healing, but to prayerfully help another. I am not able on my own. My worthiness and efforts are futile without Your sovereign grace. And yet, we both know the words on the pages must be written. You have called, and we must not let Your vineyard go untended. Lord, I'm scared. I'm scared of letting You down, afraid of not fulfilling the potential You placed within. Therefore, Lord, on the days when I don't feel You, I will need You even more. And then once again I realize, this has nothing to do with my fleshly feelings. And I sense the fleeting but so profound realization, that the very air I breathe at this moment is because of You. My pulsating heartbeat is fully known to You.

 Lord, my prayer is for You to come. Come close. Come, Lord, and let this be a season of intimacy like no other yet known by us. Let what births from this time, BLESS. Let this be a testament to Your testimony. Let these writings not be written for the approval of human's eyes or the world's light. Let the written words express the indescribable glory of You, Father God. So, my Lord God, Maker of Heaven and Earth and of my true self, be my Wondrous Weaver, for this work is Yours. Weave through this heart, mind, and earthly fingers what You desire to be written. May this book reel for another's heart to long for the essence of your Holy Spirit more than life itself. So weave. Weave threads that are fruit bearing. Spin new threads of love, light, color, and expressions of our real and authentic God. Only from the thread of True God can transformation befall. A work of the Maker's for the Master's use. This work began and continues to live through the redemptive blood and unfathomable love of The Weaver, Jesus Christ, Yourself. So begin to stitch, Lord. You make no idle loops from your needle. Take the remnants of this caterpillar and begin to weave your sacred threads into a chrysalis. I no longer choose to remain grounded. I was born for flight, and flight it must be. My wings are ready and waiting for You. It's time to take to the skies and fly.

The victory is Yours. It always has been.

Underneath Your Wing,
Nancy

Philippians 1:6

The Weaver

My life is but a weaving

between the Lord and me;

I cannot choose the colors

He worketh steadily.

Oftimes He weaveth sorrow,

and I in foolish pride

forget He sees the upper

and I, the underside.

Not 'till the loom is silent

and the shuttles cease to fly

shall God unroll the canvas

and explain the reason why.

The dark threads are as needful

in the Weaver's skillful hand

as the threads of gold and silver

in the pattern He has planned.

-Unknown

Author's Note

This book is my love letter to God, my life's expression of what the Truest King has restored. If you are reading this book, it is of God's choosing, not mine. If He felt you could glean from its pages, then let all the glory be His. I'm writing so I may never forget. Spiritual amnesia is a slippery slope. And forgetting is akin to fear. I never want to forget the depth of the pit that I was pulled from or the declaration of The Deliverer. One never wants to forget the Giver of the gift, and who gets all resplendence. Lord God, you not only saved me eternally, you saved me literally. And for this one life alone, my lips will forever praise Your holy name.

Beyond grateful I am.

To tell others of the night-and-day difference he made for you—from nothing to something, from rejected to accepted. —1 Peter 2:10 (MSG)

Section I

*An Overview
of
the Winged Journey*

Spiritual Sightings

The small winged creature was beginning to express itself in my life, with a type of heart-verbiage from the Mightiest of Vocalizers, from the very voice of God. I knew He was speaking to me in a new spirit language of sorts. God was on the cusp of creating something new. And I had been in a darkened cocoon for far too long.

Waiting for wondrous wings to awaken me to the new.

As the Monarch butterfly fluttered close by, I stood. Staring awestruck. Amazed at its coloring, positioning, demeanor … ultimately, its beauty. As the butterfly paused, I heard God speaking, revealing to me something I needed to see. My eyes were open to His voice. As the butterfly stilled itself, I also knew to "be still and know the Great I AM is God." As I lingered over another encounter, experienced on a different day, I watched its wings open and close; clapping in a sense of celebration that appeared to come over me.

And yet another butterfly sighting was completely varied. As I walked the ridge behind our mountain home, fully engaged in the music resounding from my ear buds, I was called to dance with a passing butterfly. Yes. I seized the moment and danced, with arms fully abandoned and body stretched upward toward the skies. I danced, among its glory and God's.

With each breathless beholding, a single word exploded deep within my being. TRANSFORMATION! I savored the plight of metamorphic power being displayed right before my very eyes. Wonder upon wonder was shown to me through the lens of yet another butterfly sighting. I was once again brimming with hope, promise, and belief. I knew its wings were once grounded, not even formed, so far from taking flight. A crawling caterpillar, created from egg. And through the darkness of the wondrous weave of the chrysalis, life and light emerge. I didn't want to see it leave, and yet I knew it must. For it was created for freedom, not captivity. Just like us.

And in that moment, I was so wondrously reminded of our Creator and what He is capable of doing in a life as fragile as mine.

If nothing ever changed, there'd be no butterflies.
—Unknown

CHAPTER 1

God's Most Meaningful Metamorphosis

Metamorphosis. Its meaning alone is most miraculous. I contemplate its references for further clarity and distinctness.

Metamorphosis is defined in Merriam-Webster's Dictionary and Thesaurus as "a changeover, conversion, transfiguration. A *transformation* by *supernatural* means. To change strikingly in appearance or character."

My mind wandered as I pondered the skilled hands of the Divine Weaver. Through His most ingenious mind and incomprehensible imaginative capability, He creates the brilliance of a shaded cocoon, bringing forth the emergent beauty of colorful wings.

I still marvel at this wonder.

I marvel at so many of His wonders. God enjoys enchanting us and does it amid one phenomenon after another. He provides us astounding displays as the Earth Tamer, Season Changer, Ocean Pourer, Mountain Maker, Sun Riser, Star Flinger, Hill Dresser, and Cloud Rider. All wonders of His uncontainable amazement to enjoy in this earthly time and space.

So far and wide is the vastness His creativity expresses. Just within the world of flowers, there are an estimated three hundred fifty thousand different seedlings, and in the universe of butterflies, there are more than eighteen thousand different species. Not to mention the galaxies and their stars. In the realm of astronomy, there are more than 170 billion galaxies in the observable universe. And if you multiply the number of stars by the number of galaxies, you get approximately 10^{24} stars. In layperson's terms, that is a 1 followed by twenty-four zeros. Some septillion stars. And then imagine more still. And each one being exceptional starry hosts from The Holy One!

> Ever since the world was created, people have seen the earth and sky. Through everything God made, they can clearly see his invisible qualities—his eternal power and divine nature. So they have no excuse for not knowing God. —Romans 1:20 (NLT)

In all our Maker's grand designs, Omnipotence with wisdom shine, His works through all His wondrous frame, Declare the glory of His Name.
—Thomas Blacklock

Assuredly, our finite minds can't help but be enamored with the marvelous mysteries of our infinite Creator.
Such amazing and endless wonderment surrounds us and garnishes our five senses and spirit essence!

Nonetheless, even more than experiencing and appreciating His beautiful wonders, I longed to know the Creator and the wonder of being intimately known back. Who is like The Holy? The One who marches this army of stars out each night, counting them off and calling each pinprick of light by name, never overlooking a single one. So magnificent, so powerful is He! As I pondered furthermore, I couldn't help but contemplate.

How attentively must He know, care, and watch over us?

> I look at your macro-skies, dark and enormous. Your handmade sky-jewelry, Moon and stars mounted in their settings. Then I look at my micro-self and wonder, Why do you bother with us?
> —Psalm 8:3–4 (MSG)

Therefore, I found myself caught in the spiritual eclipse of this question:

How much further still does He attend to the wild wonderment of His very own?

His own, created in His image, created to relate to His image. Could it be that you and I are the cause of His wild wonderment? For we are the ones who bear the stamp of the Creator, created from His founding fingerprints, bringing us to life to show us off as the crown of all His creatures. We are made only a little lower than the angels, bright with Eden's dawn light and a Genesis charge (Psalm 8:5–6)! He has created the vast expanse of each life, highly valuable and of an immeasurable worth. We are the sweet, sweet song. We are the once-in-all-of-history event. "We are a chosen people, a royal priesthood, a holy nation, a people belonging to God; called out of darkness into his wonderful light" (1 Peter 2:9). Chosen. Chosen with a royal status and a priestly function, called out of dark into light. Our very creation makes our occupied spot on earth a holier place.

We are His Ordained Beautifuls!

And with no debate in this truth, may we marvel even more at what becomes the Weaver's grandest of metamorphic works—bearing the most endearing of all names:

"Soul Maker"!

The shepherd and overseer of each soul

Your very soul and mine.

As I reflect on God's most meaningful metamorphosis in my life, I write in poetry.

I Stand

I stand between the years.

The former and the new,
the shadow and the light,
the false and the true,
the stationary and the flight.

I stand between the years.

So not perfected—but whole.
No longer performing—but real.
Without condemnation—but embracing.
A truer sense of self through the divine.

I stand between the years.

With tear-stained cheeks
for the inexpressible gratitude that
redemption still rings and reigns
in the Son of Righteousness.

I stand between the years.

Embracing the full meaning of Isaiah 40:31
with fresh strength and spread wings,
blackened hole replaced with sun rays,
light shining forth in illumination.

I Stand.

In wonder of the miracle itself.

And because of it,

I Stand.

I am metamorphosed in Christ my Savior. With my renewed mind, I surrender all. With my joyful heart, I praise God. With my new soul, I rejoice in my Savior.
—Alberto Casing

Why, Oh Why? The Analogy of the Butterfly

Although well over a decade past, I vividly recall the day as though it were yesterday. My excitement intensified as I began packing my bags. I was flying back to my birth state to be in my parents' home, the house I grew up in, to celebrate my mother's milestone seventieth birthday. I was looking so forward to enjoying all the invitees of her family and best of friends, as I envisioned her face surrounded by ours. We hadn't celebrated her in years. Oh, we had remembered, gifted, and celebrated her—but not in a big way, not with a party. And she was dually worthy and well overdue for such a celebration of her life.

You see, my mother's earthly battlefield was her physical health. In her youthful thirties, she was already riddled with Arthur (rheumatoid arthritis). I still remember when I was growing up, I would need to open the morning's milk carton, as her stiff and uncooperative fingers couldn't conquer the task. In her early sixties, heart disease summoned her for a (successful) open-heart quadruple bypass surgery. And then her fight with adult onset diabetes began. Its battle scars left her in a wheelchair after having her right leg amputated. And within less than two years, her left leg was also taken, leaving her with no limb to walk with. She knew pain on every realm, in ways I pray not a single one of you ever will. But never once did it define who she was. She was to be celebrated! Celebrated for her unwavering love for God and family, her admirable attitude, her persevering prayer, her selflessness, her never-ending smile, her impressive baking and cooking skills, her robust laughter, and her godly wisdom and demeanor. And not necessarily in any given order. She excelled equally in all areas. This party was to be a celebration of her essence. And in the unbridled joy of planning, I wanted a theme beautiful enough to match her worth.

With Mom's birthday falling in the latter part of the month of May, I felt that a festive spring theme of butterflies could do some justice to attracting beauty to an already enamored woman of God. I had no stronger pull to the butterfly symbol at that time than just that. I purchased butterfly plates and napkins, and even a few guest gifts would be graced to the winners who were the first to correctly answer a question concerning the life cycle of the butterfly—or if anyone in attendance was sporting a butterfly tattoo. (No luck there. But you know a party is a smashing success when the honored guest awakes the next morning with sore ribs from laughing too much.)

As soon as I arrived, Mom was eager to show me a most special gift she had already received. I was quite struck with the uncanny choice of my oldest brother Tom's gift (for both Mom and Tom were clueless of my chosen theme). It was a beautiful shadow box of mounted butterflies from all around the world! Mom's symbol of passage was being inadvertently and divinely orchestrated that day, unbeknownst to us. Only God knew this would be the last of mother's birthday parties. As one year later, He would let her soar from this earthly realm to the grandiose ascent of the Eternal City, on the wings of the mighty monarch as her symbol of passage. She still and forevermore will hold the honorary title of being the family matriarch through the beauty of the majestic Monarch.

Only in reflective understanding, have my eyes been opened to see the depth and breadth the presence of the Love Lavisher was instilling on my soul. He was already weaving a divine parallel for my own heart to embrace. Often, amid life's pain and devastation, we don't fully see.

We want to and desire to, but our own personal muck and mire often diminishes that crystal-clear view. I could only see the bud then. I now see the glory of the full bloom. The meaning of "soul metamorphosis" was taking on a new life within my own. With a graced and sharper vision, God was expressing His love to me through the parallelism between the stages of a butterfly's life cycle and my own spiritual journey. How infinitely tender His love and comradeship is. To choose this very analogy to show off His magnificence, for He already knew I yearned for the butterfly's transfiguration and flight. How could I not?

Its symbol of remembrance was of the very life that brought mine forth.

And astoundingly, although nothing is coincidental with Christ, butterflies began appearing in my life everywhere! On the front of notecards, pillow fronts, scarfs, and through living caterpillars (fulfilling their wings) gifted to me by my son Matthew and our daughter-in-love, Cari, for a special Mother's Day gift. And a dear friend, living several states away, even blessed us with a discovered monarch cocoon from her garden and brought it to my husband and I as a wedding anniversary present. With much delight, only days later, Craig and I witnessed the breaking forth of the wings and the celebration of it's first soar. Exhilarating, to watch the winged life emerge and embrace its freedom!

And the beautiful wings just kept coming. Through glass butterfly platters, hand-painted plates, and even an endearing invitation to celebrate my birthday at a butterfly pavilion, with the dearest of friends. Winged beauty was even making its way on the wall of our home. The front of our bedroom fireplace adorns a stunning original painting from an international artist (now beloved friend) of a distinguished monarch, with its most regal wingspan. Each stroke of Katherine's paint brush on the canvas was an inexpressible (surprise) gift of her love. And in this shared season, I found myself immersed with a needlepoint project whenever my hands were free and my mind needed solitude prayer. Yep—you guessed right. The completed pillow sports the stitching of the majestic Monarch. Each stitch providing still, connective, quality time with the Divine Weaver himself.

And the abundant sightings of butterfly wings in the open breeze! I was taking full notice for the first time. Each sighting became THE experience, each one as meaningful as the last. I was being graced with ingenuous eyes to savor their sacred appearance. God was speaking in theme, and He had my heart engaged. I was thunderstruck at the preference of His analogy. An analogy that began its speech from a former generation, the woman I came from. Even the Greek word for "transformed," which is *metamorphosis*, was expressed through my momma's life verse. Her all-time favorite scripture, homed in the twelfth chapter of the book of Romans, spoke of such morphing; "Do not conform any longer to the pattern of this world, but be transformed by the renewing of your mind." I was captivated by God's anticipatory love. It was much like a mother setting aside suitable gifts for her child's wedding day, even before love appears. I felt His song over me—"Will she not love this?" It became a secret love-language of intimacy between the two of us. God was showing me a treasure, and for the first time, I was finding its value. God was wrapping an extraordinary gift of redemption through the glamor of butterfly wings.

The symbolization of caterpillar, chrysalis, and butterfly represented the process that I already found myself living, working, and traveling within. I was intrigued and mesmerized by the transformative winged delight, illustrating visions of my own spiritual journey. The transfiguration of these most delicate of creatures was mirroring my current pilgrimage. This *is* "the why" for using the analogy of the metamorphic Monarch! It became imperative; its life stages needed to be the usage of explanation throughout this book. Through the shedding of my own coverings, God graced just enough courage to uncover my crippling caterpillar incapability's, just deep enough to discover a truer identity and recover a closer image of my purposed wings. Both soul and butterfly are metamorphosed. I praise, with thanksgiving full, for the witness from this intrinsic similarity. The Holy Spirit has a remarkable ability to steer our attention to divine illustrations in order to dramatize God's truths. I had no former inkling, that one of God's most delicate and smallest of creatures, weighing only .02 of an ounce, could carry such a powerful and weighty impact in demonstrating God's boundless love.

I write with more gratitude at this moment than I can fully express.

> Be faithful to that which exists nowhere but in yourself.
> —André Gide

> The privilege of a lifetime is being who you are.
> —Joseph Campbell

> I have given them the glory you gave me, so they may be one as we are one. I am in them and you are in me. May they experience such perfect unity that the world will know that you sent me.
> —John 17:22, 23 (NLT)

The Soul's Sweet Spot

Much like the mighty Monarch, we long to live in the full essence of our true creation. The *sweet spot* is where our lives glorify God within our genuine self. It's where we live out of our authentic being while granting Christ full access to spirit and soul (2 Corinthians 6:16). It's where the beauty of our true self thrives at the provision of our Heavenly Maker. It's that spiritual core that so beautifully blends True God and true self, allowing both to flourish fully, united as one. Creating an intimacy of intense, passionate, inseparable…oneness. Where the love-light of Christ lives within and shines throughout to illuminate beyond ourselves. I call this sacred space:

The soul's *Sweet Spot.*

Whether we're aware of it or not, we all desire to resemble the natural phenomenon of a caterpillar changing into a butterfly. We too want to find where our wings are meant to inhabit the skies. In that place beyond ordinary limits. Soaring closer still to the Creator's original thumbprint placed upon each life. But where do we even begin this most ardent and challenging journey? The journey of discovering our true self, a freer self, the real self, created under the wing of the Almighty.

Such a meaningful, spiritual discovery can only begin with our very creation.

Through the most loving of Creators,

God Himself.

True God — *Sweet Spot* — *Authentic Self*

Nature never repeats herself, and the possibilities of one human soul will never be found in another.
—Elizabeth Cady Stanton

I am considering not how but why God makes each soul unique. If he had no use for all the difference, I do not see why he should have created more souls than one.
—C. S. Lewis

Perfect Suit of Wings

Christ's entire affections are placed on us, with a love-purity in all its fullness. We were designed with a suit of wings that fit perfectly. Just as the twinkling of each brilliant star, the variant wing pattern on each beautifully embellished butterfly, the starlight ingenuity of each intricate snowflake, and the process of photosynthesis changing the coloring on each distinct fall leaf; *none* ever is like another. There has never been and never will be a replica of YOU. God is much too creative and expressive for that. There is far too much care and concern that went into the intricacies of your design. Nothing random here; all is spawned with extreme intentionality. Your cells were guided and governed by the most amazingly intelligent Creator. Your distinct attributes, personality, and temperament were woven by His unseen hand. Everything from the color of your eyes, hair, and skin to the demeanor of your spirit is written through divine DNA. All efforts of your individuality are designed by the High and Holy One. Brought forth and raised up …

As one's personal purposed "suit of wings".

But only for a brief second in time are we able to wear them. Only for that brief unfurling from the womb is the closest origination of self in its purest form. Its encounter is far too brief. For now, our wings have been placed in a fallen globe, where they have become misshaped, and our flight patterns of garden-purity disrupted. Each soul flutters to mimic a true image of its makings. The inescapable fallowness of fleshly nature clips unblemished newborn wings, weighing them down with earth's mud. With crooked halos and broken wings, we find ourselves flapping fervently to remain on the conquest for authentic aliveness, straining with too much self-manufactured effort, trying to escape the netted cages of our own self-imposed worlds. Our hearts long to reconnect with the clipped, orphaned parts of our truer essence and this is what *becomes* the inner quest! And in this conquest for authentic aliveness we…

Seek, Question, and Strive for:

THE ONE TRUTH.

Why is it so difficult to live from our perfect suit of wings?

Where is the belief in my own wild wonderment?

What keeps us from soaring fully alive in His love-light?

Why does the reality of living victoriously in the sweet spot of True God and true self elude us?

I've asked myself these questions about my life, pondering the priority question, seeking its truth.

Will the Soul Maker suit me with wings that fly?

There is nothing in a caterpillar that tells you it's going to be a butterfly.
—R. Buckminster Fuller

Crooked Halos and Broken Wings

We were born to fly. There is an inborn "tendency of aliveness" given to each. But full-flight wings don't come easily. Much has not developed perfectly, leaving pitted scarring on our tender human souls. Amid God's longing for each life, character, and personality to be as lovely as He visualized when He created you, earthly wings often feel somewhat amputated; causing fruitless, frustrated, and flightless spirits more often than we'd like. And stifled, stuck wings reach further depths of devastation than we dare to fully explore. So within the *heartbreak* of living out of my former fallen false self and the *heartthrob* of trusting in the transforming power of Christ to create anew …

The most intimate of spiritual journeys came calling.

I speak of it as my sacred journey of soul transformation. A journey of Thy Divine's ability to take a soul and change its appearance and character, transforming one's nature. It is the mind-blowing, boot-shaking, soul-blessing, breath-taking, humility-building, and life-altering reality of bringing a soul closer to its original creation. Transforming the fabricated self to a truer self. It's a spirit of authenticity uprising, adjoining to God's invention of it. It is the metamorphic process that God alone calls upon every soul. Courting each of us individually to surrender to The Sculptor's desired and skilled precision of His will, allowing the re-creation and restoration of our innermost parts to be brought forth as they were intended to be. It is surgical soul work! And in an attempt to summarize His most miraculous and wondrous ways;

It is the SOUL MAKER

Soul-making!

It comes in unexpected ways and at inconvenient times. It is messy, outside the lines, and includes no regimented instructional manual. This process is not something I could have mustered up myself. I don't believe I would have had the courage to do so. No formula, twelve-step program, behavioral modification technique, or reliance on my own solidified belief system was going to serve me well this time. Nor was the pulling up of my big girl boots. Muscling them to kick higher, try harder, or work faster was not going to bring about my desired wings. The supernatural feat of soul change cannot be accomplished through our fleshly efforts alone. Trust me, I've exhausted myself trying.

The "coming to" of the original blueprints placed on the womb is a spirited journey. A saturated Holy Ghost Journey. Its travels are with the Trinity Personhood at the helm, allowing the Holy Spirit to invade the soul and change it by supernatural means. It's a unique exploration, and no two paths are alike. Each individual tapestry piece of transformation is readied for the weave, by placing General Jesus in command of the colors of the threads and the pattern of the design. His spirit work comes so precisely customized when we are willing to take our hands off the loom and rely on the Weaver.

I knew I was being called to change. But before the Soul Maker could begin any surgical spiritual rehabilitation, I had to be stirred to recognize I was at a crossroads in need of transformation. I had to acknowledge that the enemy's arrows of self-denial, complacency, and fear were destroying my heart vitals. My own personal need to dig up and replant anew was inching me closer towards the top of the most urgent "list of life" for a soul transplant. Together, the Soul Maker and I needed to uproot my weedy worthlessness and discover what was real. We needed to garden in grace and then reseed. "Every plant that my heavenly Father has not planted will be pulled up by the roots" (Matthew 15:13). Such a season of breaking up the barren ground is promised. The time had come. The time was now. I was being awakened to the possibility of new life and needed to find the strength to rise from any hypnotic state or spell I had been unconsciously put under.

My inner alarm clock wouldn't stop sounding.
I was being awakened from my own enfeebling slumber.

Soul Maker,
Shake me Awake!
With a Life-Saving Shake.

Just like the butterfly, I too will awaken in my own time.
—Deborah Chaskin

Be alert, be present. I'm about to do something brand-new. It's bursting out! Don't you see it?
Isaiah 43:19 (MSG)

Wake Up, O Sleeper

No longer could I afford to be dormant, slothful, passive, or lethargic. The Soul Maker's voice had spoken and choosing to listen or not was dependent on my own self-centered free will. I knew there was no margin left to fall back asleep. Once awoken, I was fully responsible for the choice to arise. So personally private was His arousing invitation, and yet, He needed me to be a participatory player. Much like the invalid who sat by the pool in Bethesda for thirty-eight long years, I felt the Soul Maker questioning me: "Do you want to be well? Do you want to be whole? Do you want to experience the abundance that waits for you?" It was time to be proactive. It was time to advance. I felt His holy heart-tugs, telling me to get up, pick up my mat, and walk (John 5:8). To arise, leave behind any comatose condition, and carry on with an awakened soul!

May not even one of us reading this page be deceived and found foolish. For according to scripture, "the heart is deceitful above all things" (Jeremiah 17:9). It is never *if* the Soul Maker will come calling, but rather a matter of when. He's BIG in the soul-making business. Why else does His redemption cross even exist? Does the cross not encapsulate our entire purpose for being on this planet? How do we live under the freedom and fulfillment of Christ's Calvary love, as He created us to be? How can we flourish, forgiven and living further away from our sin natures, striving to overcome being victims of our false selves?

I've personally come to believe the re-finding of the original soul is the most meaningful and yet the most toilsome work a human life will undergo.

True God was cordially introducing myself to me. I needed to acknowledge, on all realms, that I was remaining in the trenches of a crawling caterpillar and experiencing its crippling effects. This revelation was necessary for the choice of freedom wings to even lie before me. I was being awoken to an escape exit out of a wilderness mentality of complacency and self-conjured creating. One that I had either been too blind or too cowardly to cross beyond its confines until now. And once its vision was revealed to me, I no longer could stay in a subconscious sluggish state.

Ephesians 5:14 is variously translated as:
"Wake up, O sleeper, rise from the dead, and Christ will shine on you" (NIV),
"Wake up from your sleep, climb out of your coffins; Christ will show you the light" (MSG).
"Wake up, you who are sleeping. Rise from the dead and Christ will give you light" (TLB).

No matter what translation is read, its message is clear. WAKE UP and Christ's light WILL Shine. It was time for my eyes to be opened to see a fuller spectrum of sight, for *awareness* alone has its way of disclosing our blindsides.

Keep your eyes open for God, watch for His works; be alert for signs of His presence. —Psalm 105:4 (MSG)

When we are blinded to our true identities, favor and freedom will *not* be granted. That's why the enemy loves to keep us comfortable. We'll remain in slumber and won't arise, seeing and believing there is more. But there always is more. Maybe that's why "He puts a little heaven in our hearts so that we'll never settle for less" (2 Corinthians 5:5 MSG).

But Satan delights when we won't pursue more, and we suffice to settle. "Keep a cool head. Stay alert. The devil is poised to pounce and would like nothing better than to catch you napping" (1 Peter 5:8 MSG). Just like our favorite recliner or a soft cushiony spot in our homes, they can be hard places to rise from. And our sluggish spiritual spaces become *the* critical places of passivity. Unfortunately, this licenses us to avoid any alert state of real awareness.

Complacency is tomorrow's Captivity!

While housing ourselves in condominiums of soul comfort, with their walls of self-protection, we are only keeping ourselves fenced in. We fall to ruin if we anticipate resting in a comfortable place. The comfort lulls us toward an "ease-disease." We then find ourselves choosing to become fainthearted victims of unwanted fears. And if we reside there long enough, it becomes a permanent residence. It's hard to fly from the nest when the cushions are made of a billowy feather-fluff, and we are well bunkered in. Even in God's order of nature, mother birds deliberately place thorns in their nests to drive their young forth toward flight. Their purposed creation is to fly. And so is ours. We desire alive flights of freedom, although it may seem easier to choose to remain tranquilized in a narcotic state of numbness. For leaving any "lodge of laziness" calls for courage. And comfort has a way of diminishing courage. An indolent spirit must vacate for victory. It is essential to arise for the sustainment of any real life.

Lord, untie our hearts and deliver us from sloth.
Discomfort us from our fallow false self.

Although we all are reluctant at times, discomfort *is* what drives us forth, breaking us out of the bondage we are in. Our passive places are what we know. And they are what is known and acceptable to others. After all, we helped create, design, and fully decorate them. But God is still sole proprietor of the original blueprints. Is not the Mighty Draftsman still the one who controls the weave from the innermost secret place of the womb? Are we allowing the Supreme Architect to build from His superlative architectural plans, or have we become our own personal designers? Fact be confirmed, there is only one set of *original* blueprints. And the Creator has full claim. Our lives are designed for His home-built habitat, one of standing on and within the Trinity Personhood. No other establishment can withstand all of time.

Craig, my husband (and beloved better half), is an established building contractor of thirty-plus seasoned years, and still reiterates: "A house is only as secure as the foundation it is built on." Hubby's words mimic the truth found in Matthew 7:26–27 (MSG)—"But if you just use my words in Bible studies and don't work them into your life, you are like a stupid carpenter who built his house on the sandy beach. When a storm rolled in and the waves came up, it collapsed like a house of cards."

Who is the foundation of your establishment? How secure is your frame? What supports your inner walls? Where does the stability of your innermost self stem from?

Stop for a moment. Press the pause button. Still the soul. And *live* the questions with God.

When we become our own builder, our small fortresses of fear and facade begin to construct coverings that were never meant to be a constructive part of the fundamental design. And through the complacency of "remaining as is", we become spiritually sedated, letting pure comfort alone lull us back to a settled slumber of unsteadiness. Satan loves to keep us stationary. This cocoon of comfort is equivalent to spiritual retirement. It is amazing how many people think their identity journey is finished. There is no retirement mode with God. We must continually be leaving our hiding places of covered, unconfessed sin and our comfort zones of being satisfied to remain as is.

It is a slow suffocation of the soul to choose otherwise.

But it's trouble ahead if you think you have it made. What you have is all you'll ever get. And it's trouble ahead if you're satisfied with yourself. Your self will not satisfy you for long.
—Luke 6:24–25 (MSG)

Suffocating in Self-Denial

If complacency alone won't lull you back to sleep, the enemy will throw his next best arrow to hijack your identity journey—the arrow of self-denial! This is huge; don't underestimate its power. What you refuse to see cannot be changed and never will be. Some hidden parts may have been with you for so long that you consider them facets of your identity, barely aware of the impact they are having on your current life. Freedom requires a *vision of truth* to move forward. At least then, opportunities present themselves with the choice for you to act upon any of His divine disclosures. What "remains as is" becomes ingrown soul-stagnation. Like painting a rundown house, the outward appearance conforms to a standard, but the inward condition remains in decay. As soon as the outward restraint is removed, the original soul state will reappear. And no matter how hard you try to cover the "unlikeables" of your inner frame …

eventually, the outer roof will begin to leak.

What starts out as a small leak, if not properly repaired, will only grow more troublesome over time. Our consciousness seeks to keep the counterfeit covered. But our subconscious revolts at the covering, and the leaking slough ultimately finds a way to have the unresolved stuff seep through. Our leaks begin to drip from improper perceptions, evaluations, even unmeant abuse from others or our own abusive self-talk. Our stuck spots seep. And each leak takes on a form all its own, appearing at unusual times and in offbeat ways. Leaks can be triggered through relationships, stress, burnout, illness, crisis, a sense of exhaustion, a feeling of emptiness, unreasonable frustration or anger, unexplainable behavior, new patterns of addiction, impatience, anxiety, sarcasm, internal uprisings, and so on and so forth.

And what do we do to stop the leaks?

We begin to plug.

We utilize plugs from our own human efforts, creating beliefs built on lies, often unaware a misbelief is even being formed. And when the improper-fitting plugs break loose, we rush to plug them again, this time maybe even using a different source that we believe will satisfy. A source that we convince ourselves may be stronger, more secure. But through the falsified coverings and unfit plugs, we only create dams. Self-willed obstructions of motionless authenticity. This unfortunately, causes a dead sea inside oneself, blocking the flow of one's own ordained vibrant life.

From the innermost being shall flow rivers of living water (John 7:38).

We are designed to be rivers, not ponds. Life is meant to be progressive, and movement is what promulgates life. Too often, we find our lily pad and stay put. It's easier to remain than to move. Just like a pond needs an outlet of water running through for freshness, we need His continual living water of life flowing through us, never leaving us as we currently are. It's the only way we will grow, stretch, and reflect more of His image in this one amazing life. Remaining as is stunts soul growth. And much like a stagnated pond, eventually the repulsive stench will begin to bleed through. Matt Chandler in *Recovering Redemption* writes, "It is okay to not be okay. It's just not okay to stay there."

It's so easy to look the other way, defy the truth, not own the responsibility, remain busy being human-doers, and not do "the work". To remain sleeping, snoozing away toward stagnant parasitic sin or self-absorption. A stagnant strain comes when we find ourselves serving another master, keeping up a personification that's not even real, not speaking truth in love, craving the good opinion of others, trying to control the outcome, or carrying two-day burdens on the one day. We are called to deal with our personal stuff. Whatever issue we don't deal with lurks alive in our heart, laying quietly down below. But in its slumber, it becomes a festering fungus of falsehood. Ignorance and suppression only multiply the spore-producing stench. And although hidden deep beneath, it will grow …

more pungent over time.

Keep a sharp eye out for weeds of bitter discontent. A thistle or two gone to seed can ruin a whole garden in no time.
—Hebrews 12:14–15 (MSG)

O Sleeper, Arise!

Don't let the little foxes in the vineyard destroy the vine.
Lord, please let the stench that bothers your heart be impressed on mine.

Awaken the parts in me that have fallen asleep.
Give me the courage to risk coming awake.

Let Your peace be my cleansing river,
carrying away the painful, poison past.

Allowing an outpouring of Your Spirit to downpour.
Ahhhhh! Like a much-awaited rain on sunbaked earth.

Its refreshment awakening me to the Rain Maker's divine dew drops,
from whom all my blessings flow.

Redirect this wayward one and refresh my weary.

To be *AWAKENED!*

> Caterpillars can fly if they only believe.
> —Unknown

> Every woman comes to a point in her life when she stops fighting against everything the world wants her to be and surrenders to everything she was born to be.
> —Unknown

The Dawn of a New Day

The dawning of God's most meaningful metamorphic process on my soul had begun. I was being invited into the very vortex of the soul, where True God introduced me to a more authentic self. It was nothing short of miraculous but felt *nothing* of the sort at the time. I felt like a disheveled snow globe being profusely shaken about and turned upside down, only to find myself in a blinding blizzard with its thick flurry of flakes swirling relentlessly. This made me feel disoriented, off-kilter, and imbalanced; far from any previous controlling forces that I trusted my own grounding to. Stinging tears were flooding my eyes. I could no longer see outward. It was time to look inward.

Inevitably, the Soul Maker tenderly brought me back to a footing, for one priority purpose—an intervention with the Timeless Truth Teller. It was a Jesus-meeting to beat all previous encounters with the Faithful and True and my faltering, false self. I needed to strip down my soul with some heavy-duty confrontation before The King. I needed to dissect with The Divine, allowing His holy written Word to divide soul and spirit, joints and marrow, to judge the thoughts and attitudes of my heart (Hebrews 4:12). I needed His powerful Word, sharp as a surgeon's scalpel, cutting through *everything*. Whether through my doubts or defense, I needed to be laid open to hear, listen, and receive the Master Surgeon's truths. It was vital for determining and dissecting the reason for my unhappiness, anxiety, depression, fear, low self-esteem, and lack of sincere joy. Once again, I found myself grateful for my upbringing, for I was raised to know there was more and who my Sufficient Supplier was!

I was meeting with the Soul Maker to begin the transformative soul-work.

> If you then, know how to give good gifts to your children, how much more will your Father in heaven give the Holy Spirit to those who ask him.
> —Luke 11:13 (NIV)

Made for More

I had been living in the lost "Land of Settlement". The place where slumber, self-denial, and Satan's lies fester together, seducing me into believing there is no more. And within the settling, my soul and spirit were dejected and felt defeated. My caterpillar legs felt heavy, far from promised lands and closer to broken promises. A slumberous weight of hopelessness kept me grounded. I was finding myself settling for less than I was brought forth to be. And my very soul was shrinking from the despair of this mistaken thinking.

But the Soul Maker always provides a way out for the Awoken One.

I praise the King with a powerful encore. For He graced me with just enough feistiness or self-inflicted fear (depending on the day or hour) that I never was too much for the settling type. In my deepest recesses, I knew there was more. I wanted MORE. I wanted the faith of our biblical friend Abraham, willing to leave everything behind to wing into the unknown (Genesis 12:1), to obey and go wherever the Father led. The choice to stay no longer held such a paralyzing grip, for the Promise Keeper keeps His promises. "You didn't leave me in their clutches but gave me room to breathe" (Psalm 31:8 MSG). A stirring deep within had already awoken me to more. I found myself recollecting words from my mother's memory, impressed on mine. My first full sentence ever spoken as a babe was "I want more" (my mother was feeding a not-yet-filled tummy). And today, in the land of the living, I still want MORE. Not more of what the world promises but more of what is promised to us, through the keepsakes of Christ. Psalm 27:13 says, "I am still confident of this: I will see the goodness of the Lord in the Land of the Living!"

I wanted the faith place of Abraham, an all-abandoned trust to follow in the footprints of The Father. I needed to surrender all five fingers on both hands, not leaving a single one unturned. I found myself longing for another instinct that comes naturally from monarch wings (unfortunately, not quite as effortless to my being.) I wanted the same trust butterflies display in their migrations. They never fear or fail to follow the wind currents. They just soar, believing their wings will be supported, knowing they are led. They are entirely confident their destination is exactly where they need to be going, even though they've never been there before. An extraordinary, uncustomary trust! As I reminded myself, "Is not the very wind held in His fists?" I found myself in prayer, pleading that my personal trek could be half as faithful as theirs, clinging onto the written words—"With faith as small as a mustard seed *nothing* will be impossible" (Matthew 17:22). No longer was settling in a suffocating slumber even an option. I was craving for His God-currents to awaken my true identity under His. I knew there was more. God always wants more for us.

And MORE is our birthright.

I pleaded for God to not leave me alone and grant me the courage to walk forth in this mystery. His written Word vowed He would do both. It took all I had on bended knee to even cry out.

But Lord, "What am I to do?"

With tear-stained cheeks, I pleaded the next question: "Where do I start?"

The Lord simply replied, "Just start."

But Lord, I am overwhelmed by the task.

He simply replied,

"But I am not."

I knew the Lord had spoken His spirit words and through the clarity of His voice,

I bowed my head.

I no longer was to remain as is.

It isn't easy to be healed. One thing is even harder though: staying unhealed.
—Philip Yancey

On the Wing of a Prayer

My fullness of time had come.

There comes a time in every life, whether recognized or not, that one no longer can remain as is. The signs will be present, but only to those who choose to be present to them. Sadly, not every person will maneuver through the maze. The question at the time was, "Would I?" My time for transformation had come, and not a moment too soon. He orchestrated the timely and necessary intersection. He often does His finest work in the eleventh hour. I now realize I was living in the eleventh hour, and the sand in the hourglass was barely visible. A mere blur of an authentic being was fading fast through the glass. I had become a self-manufactured soul by my own power and means. My reality of "being" was no longer working for me. My cracked recesses of self-hatred and falsehood were beginning to shatter. My time to wholly break was beckoning. I needed just enough gut-level grace to find the courage to accept the risk of giving up all the pieces and putting away my own bottle of mismanaged gorilla glue. It was my only chance of becoming a closer collective beauty of who I was birthed to be. If I didn't go forward this time, would I ever? His opportune upheavals are for reasons far beyond our earthly watches, saturated schedules, and human comprehension. Beyond doubt, His timing and resolution are always divinely precise and shockingly purposeful! Remaining as is comes with much too high of a cost. I know. I had remained for more of my life than not. And the price of remaining almost cost me my life.

I ached to live within my own personal wonderment for the display of His splendor. Anything else was inauthentic living. And through this most impassioned journey, I begin to clearly see that counterfeit living may well be …

the greatest human tragedy in any given life.

In hindsight, I look back upon these seasons for what they truly were. Forever will they be my greatest of gifts from the Giver of Life. I was being carried under His Almighty Wing and the wing of many a prayer.

It was in this season when He took this broken soul and literally saved it from itself.

God is the power behind your metamorphosis. We don't have the power to make lasting changes in our lives. That's why we must rely on God's strength to transform us. As we enter the path of transformation, the most valuable thing we have working in our favor is our yearning.
—Cynthia Bourgeault

If being a beggar in spirit is a form of yearning, I had plenty.

I was forced to go deeper or die.

My life was unraveling into something unforeseen and unknown to me, and yet, I knew God was calling me to follow the pain or not survive. I was on the heels of the birth of our most beautiful and beloved second son, and although the world wanted to write it off as post-partum depression, I knew it was deeper, more intense, and of a greater spiritual nature, encapsulating my entire holistic nature and taking all realms of my physical, emotional, and mental entities, along with my spirit. I no longer was mine. I had grown too far from my original self to even know how to return. There was a stifling of true self that needed to be reborn, remade in His image. My fabricated self no longer fit. No matter how hard I tugged and pulled to have my wings appear to fit properly, the discomfort was growing unbearable.

Just like the blessed butterfly wiggling to break free from the cocoon, the timing is graced and given. The choice will present itself, when greater life must come forth. And the decision to grow rests fully on our willingness to choose. I was being led to leave behind my legs of creeping caterpillar (thanking them for their support but no longer wanting the earthen crutch they provided) and felt sheer fear in the foreignness of letting them go. The removal of my fabricated existence needed to leave its husks somewhere, never to be found again. I knew I was on the brink of something so much bigger than I. I was being introduced to an uproar of uneasiness I had never before experienced and didn't even know existed. The utter darkness of the deep black hole was not lifting.

Life had become what John of the Cross once referred to as the "dark night of the soul." Filled with an all-encompassing world of soul determent, I was fading fast. My intermittent panic attacks were the result of growing allergic to my false self, and its anxiety was choking me to death. I was beginning to isolate and reject myself. Feelings of alienation and separation assailed me. Henri J. M. Nouwen said, "Self-rejection is the greatest enemy of the spiritual life because it contradicts the sacred voice that calls us the 'Beloved.' And being 'His beloved' constitutes the core truth of our existence."

Once a former social butterfly, I was now experiencing full-blown agoraphobia. And I was willing to do almost anything to stop feeling the fear and the fear of the fear of another attack. I don't know if you've ever experienced panic attacks, but I equate them as my greatest earthly torment. There is not another feeling I despise more than that of intense fear. On certain days, I didn't even want to leave the confines of my front door and found the Lord's experienced power demonstrated through my first memorized scripture: "I can do all things through Christ who strengthens me" (Philippians 4:13). Never did His faithful word fail to escort me on. I no longer could make the pieces fit or try to hold them in a place of pretentious appearance.

The weeks turned into months.

As the flower and butterfly desperately need each other for survival, my life was growing more urgently dependent on His!

I was finally right where He needed me to be.

At the end of myself.

The end of your rope is the beginning of God's doorstep.
—George Muller

The strongest position you can be in is complete surrender.

Life is a balance between what we can control and what we cannot control. I'm learning to live between effort and surrender.

Transformation happens on the other side of surrender.

Soul Surrender

Through the mere bliss of sacred surrender alone, my image in the mirror was beginning to exhibit teeny, tiny tidbits of transformation. And I do mean tiny. But I was trusting in their positive transfigurations, even though there were still canyon-deep crevices in need of counsel. I no longer was exhausting myself in my own efforts. This designed dependence graciously drew me closer to the Soul Maker. For my gaping, open-wounded spaces could only be rectified and redeemed through the Solitary One. The only thing I was in control of was my knees.

Surrender is a journey from outer turmoil to inner peace.

I found myself recalling words spoken to me years ago, from a faithful pastoral friend—"There are two teachers in life, Wisdom and Pain." And since in this juncture of my journey, I could only find myself experiencing my own blackened feelings, my full-throttle pain took precedence. There is nothing like the promptness of what feels like unalterable pain to drive a woman to her knees a bit more readily, than waiting on what seemed like unobtainable transfiguration through given wisdom, to take its firm hold.

Only God knew the depth of my despair. I was clueless about the spiritual journey I was going to embark upon and with an intensity never before acquainted to me. But as we all know, God loves us far too much to keep us as we currently are. My time had come. I was ripe for the picking and in need of greater chosen fruit. Was I willing to join in and engage in His unseen plans? Was I willing to leave all behind to follow? Would the much-needed courage come to me for the freefall from the great oak of my own growing? As the saying goes, "When the student is ready, the teacher will come." My pain had grown greater than the risk. I needed to ready myself to move. I needed to fully surrender. To utterly, yield. There is nothing more powerful than a surrendered life in the hands of God. For what is given through submission, He takes and multiplies by His power. I heard His voice speaking through His own red-letter words (Matthew 4:19):

"Come, follow Me."

When God gives a command or a vision of truth, it is never a question of what He will do, but what we will do. —Henrietta Mears

I prayed fervently for an ounce of courage to choose the change! No longer could I skirt around the upheavals of my heart. My relentless pain was pulsating for whatever it was going to take for some relief. I needed to forge forward to face what I had not been strong enough to bear before. I needed soul rehabilitation from my own blind-sided sin, fleshly desires and distractions, insecure self-reliance, and my dis-ease to please. My very life depended on my trek out of my own self-created Egypt. My escape to Canaan was growing non-negotiable. Desperately and inevitably, my time for soul-detoxing had come. My awakening for the supernatural became life-sustaining (or potentially life-ending). I needed a power far beyond self. I needed the God of Angel Armies, the Living Source of All Capability, and the Lifter of my Head and Holder of my Heart. My heart's cry had never been more real to His ever-attuned ears. I ached with the same scripted words of Psalm 34:6: "With all my might I shout up to God, His answers thunder from the holy mountain." I lamented and longed for the One and Only, my Altar Rock! Desperation plus faith is a powerful combination.

With a solo word of pure anguish, I cried out,

"COME!"

And

He came.

We are never left alone when we are at our poorest.

The cry of the human soul never goes unheard from the Soul Maker.

> But they did not listen or pay attention; instead they followed the stubborn inclinations of their evil hearts. They went backward and not forward.
> —Jeremiah 7:24 (NIV)

Pay Close Attention

My journey was well underway, but it wasn't just the surface layer that needed tending to. Our souls are much like the peels of an onion, stripping the next layer in their graced time. He knew fully what I could receive and allowed me a restful reprieve when I was not yet ready for the growth of a holier harvest. Together, we began doing the work—uprooting, weeding, tilling the barren soil to bear new seed. And I was discovering the challenging aspects of growing new wings. They not only take time, they also involve growing pains.

Transformation without work and pain is just an illusion of true change.
—Paul Young

Transformation is not a magical wand, never a onetime shot. It is progressive, continual. And just when I thought a lesson was learned from the Loving One, another layer deeper down was divulged. I find, through the Greek word for transformation, these revealing scripture words: "So we are transfigured much like the Messiah, our lives gradually becoming brighter and more beautiful as God enters our lives and we become more like him" (2 Corinthians 3:18 MSG). This scripturally shows us that our spiritual growth is always a continual, lifelong process. More threads in this chrysalis will be needed for each spiritual spin. Much like the morphing process from caterpillar to abundant wings, I also needed in-between stages of space and time to implement the transformation that set me free to soar to the next new height.

I could hear Him speaking over me, "Be patient, My child. I am doing a new thing."

And I would find myself back in the chrysalis again, back to another yet different stuck spot, but purposefully bringing a bit more vibrant color to the wings each time I entered in.

I didn't mind the time frame of His faithful works,
as long as the Soul Maker attended.

The Soul Maker always ATTENDS. He is never voiceless to those who choose to hear. Had my soul grown inattentive and insensitive? Was I the one growing deaf? Was I losing Him through the subtle ways of simple inattention? Ignored inner-spirit souls will take a downward spiral if left on their own. It was clear, He was summoning my attention now! And it enthralls me how He reaches us. I remain awestruck how the Lord could use a simple phone call to have such a powerful effect on the course of my life. No, it wasn't a diagnosis from a doctor or life-shattering news about a loved one (although I have painstakingly experienced both), but the call came with a match-full intensity that held a much more valuable meaning then I first thought. This call was of a different kind. This was a call from the Creator, literally awakening me to save my own life. It was a call that asked me to lay down my current life, surrender what was and what I knew, and enter a foreign land unknown to me. It allowed His transformative touch to whittle away, creating a truer identity through the craftmanship of His bladed knife.

I didn't want to miss out on the furtherance of His shavings of becoming real, although it raised some questions: How real am I? What illusions have I created? What parts of me are not of His design?

We are not very good at recognizing illusions, least of all the ones we cherish about ourselves. —Thomas Merton

We're containers filled with an ego elixir we've brewed ourselves. —Sue Monk Kidd

The Soul Maker has His ways of arousing our attention when He is ready to whittle. The phone call came on a Thursday morning from an acquaintance, someone I met only weeks prior in a training course. Although, now decades later, I can't even recall her name, I'll never forget her message. She was the Lord's chosen emissary, and her divine assignment of delivery came on the purity of angel wings. She shared the following through the voice message recorder: "Nancy, I was led to pray for you today. God asked me to relay three things to you." Now that's quite a proclamation for anyone! Never before or since has this happened to me. She calmly spoke the following:

1. God wants your attention.

2. You are "doing."

3. God wants you to "be."

I sat for a few brief moments and pondered the message. In my prideful arrogance, I thought I could clearly decode God's message to me. Simply put, I was too busy and needed to slow down. Oh, how miserably incorrect and shallow my thinking was. God grew me to see the true revelation of the phone message. He was calling me to be closer to the original thumbprint He placed on my life. God wasn't calling me to slow down. He was calling me into the depths of true transformation. Only in retrospect, have I grown to see how incredibly different the two understandings are.

And the timing of this message proved to be just as relevant. It came at a time in my life when the winter of the soul once again wrapped me in its cold, uncomfortable cloak. I had been diagnosed with Spasmodic Dysphonia, a rare neurological disorder where the vocal cords close involuntarily. If He needed my fullest of attention, He had it then. For those who know me well, you would most likely agree, I am in the 90 plus percentile as an enthusiast who adores words, whether written or verbal. Now this calls for crucial information to fully understand the impact of my signal. For there was no greater way to apprehend my full attention, stop me dead in my tracks, and compel me to mercifully look up than to have a malfunctioning larynx. God shapes each of us primarily to be talkers, feelers, thinkers, or doers. Each arena is God-ordained. Talkers are heart people and have a hard time being quiet. When you're a heart person, you've got to express it. You love connecting with souls. Talkers love to sit and converse, especially in heart-to-heart conversations. It's a most favorite thing to do. Hmmm, Life Coach…could be why? According to test results from a Taylor-Johnson Temperament Analysis Profile, my highest ranking was a score of 98 percent in the Expressive-Responsive traits: spontaneous, affectionate, demonstrative. Its opposite shows inhibited traits of being restrained, unresponsive, and repressed. Not so much myself. Enough said. I'm only sharing for its purposeful point. My sign unsettled me more than another possibly could.

I was now unable to speak fluently. Its impact was enormous. This physical condition was affecting my work and every single aspect of my life. From a short phone conversation to ordering off a restaurant menu, I felt helpless as I struggled with my own voice box. I felt such great despair through this sense of helplessness. It's often on the underside of our tapestries of life where we become most aware of His presence. He knows how to ready each soul for ripening and brings us to His full attention when we need to be present to it.

My sign was now in place.
An altered, stuttering form of speech.

I hated my sign. But nothing comes to us that God will not use for great purpose. And thank goodness, His most creative power surges at the point of our helplessness. Could this brokenness be a lighthouse in disguise; beckoning me for what the subconscious spirit possibly may no longer want to keep silent? It was time to reclaim my authentic inner voice and give it back its rightful position and power, starting with my need to choose an improved lens of hope to look through. Our signs are never meant to be our foes. Life's afflictions can often be our refining-fire friends. They carry great potential to be the proponents we've been (sometimes unknowingly) waiting for.

Becoming our very gateways to deliverance!

Our brokenness can be trained to behave, but only momentarily. When things start to unravel, we need to pay attention. God is bringing forth an opportunity, an opportunity to see Him, an opportunity to walk intimately with Him, an opportunity to break free. To the alert Christian, interruptions are divinely injected opportunities. When we are falling apart, could it be the Great Encourager's chance to let everything fall together?

What was God's message for me within this interruptive chaos?

A wondrous, opportune uprising toward authenticity!

Again, we are complex, multifaceted, holistic creatures of mind, body, spirit, and soul. Whether through relational issues, emotional upheavals, or tiny trigger points that set off anger, jealousy, lustful desires, addictions, and yes, even physical ailments; God is calling us to pay attention. And though it may not feel like the truth, God's graciousness *is* being delivered within the disruptive and destructive signs. Adversity can unmask us and change us all at the same time, if we allow it. I was feeling bruised, bloodied, and broken again. I beckoned for another arm wrestle, begging to understand and make some sense out of this unwelcomed, painful scenario. I wanted to wrestle well, like Jacob. I wanted to come out winning. Even if I walked away with a limp, this was one of those solitary times I needed to question, argue, and assimilate my soul with the Solitary One.

I hated the signal given to me,
and yet I somehow knew the Soul Maker would bless the broken road.

He always does.

Perhaps strength doesn't reside in having never been broken, but in the courage required to grow strong in the broken places. —Kristen Jongen

For in Him we live, and move, and have our being. Acts 17:28 (NIV)

Just Be

There is a huge difference between existing and LIVING. Living comes through Beingness. And this book is about "being", being Authentically ALIVE in Christ! I believe you will find its meaning to be more profound than it may first appear on this page. For if not, I have faltered in my expression to explain well. This book is a collective read of thoughts, prayers, visions, poems, teachings, quotes, and scriptural truths on the topic of beingness. Our being is the authentic spirit we were birthed with, under the weavings in the womb. It is the "light site" where His glory shines forth with the originality of Himself, the central essence of who we truly are.

We are born to be human beings, not human-doers. Our being encompasses our accomplishments, our works, and our doings, but it's not solely the essence of our core. When roles are removed, and responsibilities stripped, what remains within? Who are you then? What lies underneath the tasks, hats, good deeds, and masks is the living soul. Our servanthood is important, but not before we have our being awoken to its proper placement. For all life-spirit flows from its center. Its essence is realness, richer than performance, posture, purpose, or service. It is who we are in our core nature, not so much what we do in career or service, that brings prestige, power, or position. But what brings sincere peace, radiant joy, and internal freedom.

From our beingness, *all* wellspring of life emerges.

Our life is much more than fulfilling our purpose, although there is great merit in that. Don't get me wrong here. Purpose is of *much* importance. After all, I am a Purpose Life Coach for heaven's sake. But through my coaching career, I began to realize more fully that if our understanding of God and believing in our identity in Him is not firmly planted, it's more difficult to find our "light site" that displays His shine or our unique place of joyful purpose. Only from knowing God and understanding Him can we experience our true identity. Our unique aliveness, spiritual centering, potential, creativity, motives, character, passions, demeanor, lightship, and legacy all come out of our beingness. Allowing the me to flourish from a purer place. This gives truth to our earthly vessel, as we live more authentically centered within the sweetest of spots. For when we live outside of our sweet spot, we often are overly striving or incompletely being. A sure sign of over-striving can bring feelings of being burnt out or even bitterness from the busyness that is necessary to keep all the plates spinning. We may begin to feel overwhelmed, with no real joy found in the service, helps, or works. Alive souls are rarely burdened with burnout, at least not as a core issue. But the more criminal of cases is when we rust out, for this reflects our under-beingness, selling ourselves short of our true worth by never believing, discovering, or living from our uniqueness. Both are crushing to our potential.

Alive-living comes out of being in real identity.

The health of the soul presides the fullness of service.

Identity before Activity.

We have it backwards. Our being must precede our doing and consuming if we are to grow up into all the fullness of Christ.
—Jane Rubietta

If we don't know who we are in Christ, it will not only affect where we go and what we are willing to attempt for God, it will also affect the efficiency of God's very expression within our actions. A very sobering thought, I know. Our truest purposes can only be lived through our authentic beings. False identity journeys are distorted and constantly become derailed. We find our journeys hijacked; whether by others' labels, roles, agendas, or opinions or by our own negative self-talk and mistaken thinking. Staying true to self and who God says we are must be greater than the world's pull. We don't want to just blend in, get by, or serve for the self-lifting charge we receive from our own sainthood.

Our beingness is ultimately the expression of His light!

This life is the one chance to be YOU! Your being is the original, unique, never-to-be-found again "expression of self" for His glory! We need to become our rightful self through the Righteous One. It's your one life to shine your light. No other can match, surpass, or wear its forming from the womb. It is your one true being. There is so much within you yet to unwrap. Live yourself enthusiastically. You are filled with His awesomeness! Your gift of self is what you give back to the Giver of Life and all He places in your path. Let your light shine. Let it shine *brilliantly, boldly,* for all to see.

Be a Light-Bearer on your Graced Hilltop!

You're here to be light, bringing out the God-colors in the world. God is not a secret to be kept. We're going public with this, as public as a city on a hill. If I make you light-bearers, you don't think I'm going to hide you under a bucket, do you? I'm putting you on a light stand. Now that I've put you there on a hilltop, on a light stand—shine! Keep open house; be generous with your lives. By opening up to others, you'll prompt people to open up with God, this generous Father in Heaven. —Matthew 5:14–16 (MSG)

I love people and the uniqueness of their own light. Truly, you are the best of gifts to unwrap and open. So much beauty to discover and enjoy. Your life matters grandly. And I have a sincere passion for another's flight toward freedom too. My one and only God-graced and unprecedented sister, Shari, calls me a "freedom-fighter", not just for my own soul but for the sake of others. It may be why I love heart connections. I love to see another's light in Christ radiantly alive, illuminating onward. And I've grown to learn through my own travels and those around me that believing, recognizing, and holding your light is what brings forth the freedom wings.

I'd love to share a few examples of freedom wings through clientele (it's a perfect opportunity to showcase their light). Glori Ann came looking for her unique identity. She felt she was living safely under the shadows as her husband's wife and children's mother (her greatest of joys), but she wanted to meet herself. She chose to paint a picture as we journeyed. She painted a picture of a lion in a sandstorm, its mane fighting the adversity of the wind as its paws were kept hidden underneath the blinding sand. This image beheld the vision of her own bravery, as she proceeded onward, uncertain of where her own feet were leading her. She called her painting *The Courageous One*. She found her stronger, truer self under the Master Painter's brush.

And Lois's light came forth as she longed to fulfill a vacated dream. She began attending voice lessons (while raising her little ones) to outwardly express her love for God within. She performed at a CD release event, to a sold-out hall, later that year. Her CD, entitled *A Rose in Winter*, found her back to her footed faith.

And Danica found freedom wings to leave behind her seventy-hour work weeks as a financial analyst to discover her God-giftedness. Danica was born with an eye to capture beauty. Whether through the expressions and spirit of people, the scenery, or the personality of each unique soul, she was gifted with sight to see the Spirit. She is an extraordinary photographer and loves her life today. She has been graced with a vision to see the love of God in all around her.

Each of these women are great examples of exuding their light-site. Under the Lightship of Christ!

And a word of cautionary insight. We must never give any earthly person control or power over our light. No one else is qualified to be a critic. Only the Eternal Blazing Lamp gets to weigh in on our authentic life. Our authentic self should never be pushed or asked to be altered or suppressed in any way. If we are being asked to change the essence of self to meet the needs or comfort of another, it may be their opportunity to look within themselves and do their own soul work. Impatient demands, lack of acceptance, or judgment placed over another's true light is their issue of change, never your own. May we always find ourselves looking for the good in others and growing with acceptance in understanding the differences. Acceptance creates a safe place to be and experience ourselves and others. We need to be able to share our complete self, whether good, bad, broken, happy or healed. Judgment carries threads of disharmony. And discord is enemy territory, and he will latch on and run with it every time. "Let no bitter root grow up to cause trouble and defile many" (Hebrews 12:15b

NIV), for it will sprout like a little wicked weed. And if not pulled up by its root, it will creep and infest all in its path, overshadowing even the deepest Christian relationships with jealousy, disappointment, and dissension. Our great spiritual task is to fully trust that we belong to God—free to speak and give even when our words or gifts may not be received, and free to act when we are criticized or asked to suppress. (And we all know the difference between constructive criticism and the sting of judgmental criticism.) We need to live, experiencing we are fully loved by God beyond any opinion objecting otherwise.

> When you fear you aren't enough or that you're too much—you really fear the freeing beauty of being you.
> —Ann Voskamp

Whether it be through an assessment of not being enough or being too much, remember that we are godly ones, with grace and discernment. We want more than anything else for the Jesus within to be seen. And He graces us with the ability to monitor our dimmer switch, if need be. We don't want to be found hiding our light under a bushel or burning another with our lamp's oil. Be considerate of other people's vibrations of you; ask God to give you mature wisdom to know how to handle certain situations and relationships. Even Jesus and His disciplines were shunned for their light. And when they were not welcomed in a home or city, they had to shake the dust off their feet and leave (Matthew 10:12–15 shares this scenario). Raw truth—sometimes you need to accept that you'll never be acceptable enough for some people. Be discerning, graceful, and kind. But never shun your own inner light. It is your essence. It is your beingness. And it exhibits the very glory of God.

> For our authentic self has an inner lighthouse, knowing where to best shine the beacon.

And we must stand shielded against any opposition of its brightness.

So to exude authentic light, we need to travel past the permissions of other people or their expectations to back down or change a truer self. If we let the judgment of others stop us from being real, causing us to live guarded, we no longer are ourselves. We become someone everyone else wants us to be. This may be pleasing to them but tragically unauthentic to self and your glorious creation. Watch for the signs. If you find yourself exerting too much energy toward another to satisfy them, you are compromising a part of yourself, possibly revealing that you may be struggling to maintain healthy boundaries or seeking to fill inner cisterns from empty wells.

Both are colossal light-destroyers.

And your candle is far too brilliant
not to fully shine!

Your spirit is the sunshine; your soul the stained-glass window it shines through. —John Eldredge

Love yourself enough to set boundaries. Your time and energy are precious. You get to choose how you use it. You teach people how to treat you by deciding what you will and won't accept. —Anna Taylor

Boundaries define us. They define what is me and what is not me. A boundary shows me where I end and someone else begins, leading me to a sense of ownership. Knowing what I am to own and take responsibility for gives me freedom. —Henry Cloud

Boundaryless Brooks and Empty Wells

Boundaries are a blessed imperative to holding the luminosity of your lighthouse. Boundaries are meant to keep us safe and protected in healthy, loving relationships. Now, I'm talking wholesome boundaries here, not walls of self-protection that keep us locked out, in, and away from a more authentic life. Without sound boundaries, our lives become chaotic. We begin running around like Chicken Little, trying to meet the demands of this world or the demands we place on ourselves.

Boundaryless living is not a breaking-free lifestyle.

And faith wings can't evolve in their forming or soar freely within this altered state.

Bubbling brooks of boundarylessness can appear at any time. Even within secure borders, small hairline fractures can flare up. And much like bones within the body, hairline fractures can cause pain and havoc. They eventually become dividing lines of invasive injury, in need of healing. A lack of boundaries comes from trying to fill faulty needs, with unhealthy motives, through false means. And you may find it easier to see in others, overlooking yourself. We often can have ingrown eyeballitis toward our own boundaryless mess, especially when we allowed its artful innovation through means of our own making.

Boundaryless borders are discovered and (healed) by considering the motive of the true heart's intent. And when we seek the Great Revealer, He will bring light and weight to our motives.

All a man's ways seem innocent to him, but motives are weighed by the Lord. —Proverbs 16:4 (NIV)

He will bring to light what is hidden in darkness and will expose the motives of men's hearts.
—1 Corinthians 4:5 (NIV)

Revealing and bringing truth to the motives that drive the decisions behind our yeses and no's is imperative to healing identity-work. If we are striving, pleasing, controlling, or compromising out of a position to feed prideful egos, squelch insecurities, or sacrifice self for another's approval, or ignoring our current life status by being too involved in another's, we are not "freedom girls". It can be hard to see our own boundaryless mess because we fuel it through empty cisterns of our own choosing. And we often go back to the same pump for each artificial refill. Injecting our soul tanks with false fuel, leaving us running on empty.

I began to more fully understand and implement healthy boundaries through my profession before looking even closer at my personal life. I was learning that I could encourage and care for clients without carrying them. Their work was theirs, not mine. I needed to let their journey be just that—theirs! I could instruct, pray, bless, and then release them. The Ultimate Life Coach, Christ, is always the true source and guide. We are merely the conduits. I had to go through an entire season of just learning this one simple action. It's God's work, in His way, through His life, in His time. I sometimes still stumble in this area, wanting something so badly for someone who is not ready to receive it (or may not even be in need). The last thing we need is to be a little god in another's life—thinking we know what is best and growing frustrated with what we may see as their lack of progress. Christ is really the Great Uncoverer. Others, only conduits. And this frees us to be responsible for only ourselves.

We are never responsible for other people's happiness, as they are not responsible for ours. This secures us to be "People Releasers". Secure people release others to discover, obtain, and express their true identities and faith journeys, as they will. And it's liberating for both parties when we allow each other to be responsible for dealing with our own stuff. We can be springboards of encouragement and belief for one another, praying and pointing each other upward to the True Source as we allow the journey to be more a walk beside The Weaver. He knows the stitch better than any other. May we find ourselves entrusted in good measure to uphold His pattern as the primary path to follow.

How influential my clients are to me. When I challenge them, I contest myself. They teach me much. As they were discovering the hairline fractures of boundarylessness in their lives that caused barren wasteland, I began to see fault lines within my own borders. And I'd like to share a few examples of unhealthy boundaries that most people have likely experienced at some point. For example, when has intimidation caused you to back down? When do good deeds cross over into self-glorifying acts? When does bullying bring you under their control? When does the prayer concern for another get squashed through the loose lips of gossip or judgment? When does someone's expectation cause you to jump to their demand? When do you find yourself changing your stance to appease another, ignoring your own soul-self? Or when does someone's choice to not affirm your growth cause you to wilt back down to a level of mediocrity again? These are all ways of creating hairline fractures of false and boundaryless living. And they create the potential for spidery webs of netty relationships, entangling all who get caught in its interlace. And once a levee on a boundaryless brook breaks, it can be hard to regain what could have been a cherished relationship.

This led me to address the boundary issues of my heart, which were becoming a bit agitating in my own spirit. My irritating issues were really arguments within myself. And if a relationship is starting to show boundaryless activity, it is our position to bring it back in balance.

When we sense small pushes against our walls (or recognize ourselves pressing in against another's) take note of how it makes you feel. If you are being made to feel guilty, bullied, judged, manipulated, or a bit shoved, look at what is taking place. And if you are finding it challenging to maintain a strong fringe, it is time to take heed. We need to examine what is truly taking place. If something isn't sitting right with your spirit, take notice. We may be allowing another to infiltrate our perimeters. How can we stand in accord of the Worthy One if we cannot take a stand for our own worth?

If something is not sitting right in your spirit, Stop.
Realign the relationship right from the onset.

Lord, give us wisdom and help us recognize when our lives are out of balance; summons within us the courage to correct it.

Boundaries are always for our betterment and for God's glory, for even God wasted no time in showing us the importance of necessary boundaries from His Beginning Garden. God created a decisive boundary against eating the forbidden fruit. And, oh my, look what happened after the apple-eating incident—the fall of all humankind!

I confronted with The King about the abrasive surfaces I was experiencing. He showed me my boundaryless brooks, which were never meant to satisfy. I began to instill a couple of sturdier stakes around my own banks, making me breathe a little lighter. I no longer needed to be anyone else's happiness or they mine. We savored, enjoyed, and rejoiced in what we were graced with together, without needing to be space invaders. Requesting, needing, or demanding more from another are the hairline fractures to take a closer look at, for fault lines gone awry only show us areas of emptiness within ourselves. When relationships become a bit boundaryless, seek the truth of the situation. Then, dry up the brook before it spills over its banks, building a false idol of continual emptiness, only drowning us deeper in a sea of loneliness. Washing us farther out into the uncharted waters of unauthenticity.

Boundaryless brooks can easily lead to empty wells.

We all have "wells", bottomless pits where we attempt to satisfy our thirst. And they are our ATTACHMENT DISORDERS! For we are connecting to a falseness to fill. They can be ourselves, others, the world, even religion. Yes, even religion. If we are striving for sainthood through religious good deeds, we miss out on the more important thing; relationships. As Matt Chandler writes, "A system of thought where people perform certain acts or rites or scheduled ceremonies, hoping to keep their accounts paid up so they can one day turn in their chips for final redemption, is *not* freedom."

This world and the things of it will never satisfy. We all tried, just like King Solomon. There is no new thing under the sun and nothing here that will fulfill. Our happiness will never be found drinking from empty cisterns of half-truths for happiness. Their false fill will leave us parched. There is only One Thirst Quencher that flows with an everlasting supply of love and satisfaction. His name is Jesus. Anything else is a counterfeit of contentment. And we all come thirsty. Where are you finding your steadfast stream of water that quenches?

> It's impossible to fill an empty bucket with a dry well.
>
> There is only one well, the Water-of-Life Well,
>
> which holds an endless depth of satisfaction.
>
> Our thirst coupled with our faith
>
> leads us beside the Quiet Water Replenisher
>
> who restores each thirst-deprived soul
>
> with His everlasting cup of contentment.
>
> Always runneth over and never runneth dry!

Then He said, "It's happened. I'm A to Z. I'm the Beginning, I'm the Conclusion. From the Water-of-Life Well, I give freely to the thirsty." —Revelation 21:6 (MSG)

There is trouble ahead when you live only for the approval of others, saying what flatters them, doing what indulges them. Popularity contests are not truth contests—look how many scoundrel preachers were approved by your ancestors! Your task is to be true, not popular. —Luke 6:26 (MSG)

I needed to stop placing the responsibility of who I was in the hands of someone else. As a former professed people-pleaser, I needed to put down my cup of preoccupation with what others thought of me and replace it with a toast to the Highest of Holies for my identity found in Him.

To continue to draw water from a dry oasis is DANGEROUS!

Boundaryless brooks and empty wells are the unfortunate ways we live under the law and not grace (Romans 6:14). We can never earn enough to make ourselves worthy. Otherwise, redemption is founded on what we can do, not on what has already been done for us. It's all about His grace in, over, and around us.

Father God, Water-wash us in Your amazing grace!

A tumbling waterfall of grace.

Amazing, amazing grace.

GRACE.

How Sweet the Sound that Saved a Wretch like Me!

I do not at all understand the mystery of grace—only that it meets us where we are but does not leave us where it found us. —Anne Lamott

Grace is the only thing that is ever enough. —Ann Voskamp

'Tis Grace that brought me safe thus far; and Grace will lead me home. —John Newton

Garlanded in Grace

How do we define the emotion or create an emoji for grace? Yes, I love my phone's emojis. (Aj, it's all your fault; chuckles, my friend.) We know the definition for *grace* is "unmerited favor; an undeserved kindness." But how does grace feel? How is grace experienced? How does the soul define grace?

I was spending a very special girlfriends' get-away weekend in Taos, New Mexico. Sarah was going to be a bride in a few weeks, and she wanted to spend this weekend intentionally prepping her heart for her soon-to-be husband. Throughout the weekend, I thought often of our biblical sister Esther. Sarah's intentions reminded me a bit of Esther's preparations before she went before the king—cleansing, purifying, praying, and listening. Sarah desired to hear from the Lord as her pen romanced her journal.

Sarah's chosen weekend retreat get-away included a full day at an outdoor spa frilled with healing mineral pools, hammocks, and adobe fireplaces. Signs were posted to limit use of cell phones and to keep voices to soft whispers. The resort was nestled in a majestic mountain scene. Awwwww Calgon, take us away! The ambiance beckoned for reconnecting to all that really matters—silence, solitude, and nature's backdrop of serenity. We exhaled worldly ways and inhaled stillness. This was an oasis of tranquility, where our daily supplements consisted of a generous dose of fresh air, vitamin D from the sun, and restful soul time with the Truest Son. The best of holy-healing agents!

We rose early with anticipation and prepared for our spa day with a healthy breakfast, exercise, and a time of gathered prayer. As I was preparing breakfast, I couldn't help but notice our weekend adobe dwelling's refrigerator, which displayed the following written in mini-magnet bites:

> Grace/is/a/divine/miracle/beyond
>
> the/highest/sunlit/waterfall
>
> a/white/gossamer/blossom
>
> shining/amidst/invisible/paradise
>
> a/starry/night/twinkle/ing
>
> within/a/silken/crystal/evening
>
> a/glorious/morning/sanctuary
>
> emerge/ing/like/iridescent/wave/s
>
> an/eternal/mountain/meadow
>
> across/heavenly/precious/earth
>
> travel/ing/home/toward/freedom
>
> I so appreciated the attempt to describe grace.

GRACE!

Some words just scream for skin on them.

I pondered the feeling of grace.

Grace.

Special words only gain meaning when they have "experience" to them.

I viewed the last sentence of the mini magnets.

"Traveling home toward freedom."

Of Course!

The feeling of grace is FREEDOM!

We inhale and exhale more effortlessly under the breath of grace.

We drink differently under the goblet of grace.

We live more fully alive,

Wrapped in His blessed bonds of garlanded grace!

Our beingness grows through seeds of grace. It doesn't come from striving or works of our own self-will. Although we are called to be participatory players, it is His garlands of grace that provide, protect, and pave the way. The time of getting real under grace was becoming my reality. I was discovering the WHO in the real me, within a beautiful exchange of intimacy with the Awesome God of All Wonders.

A journey on graced wings.

I no longer needed to posture, perform, or strive to be better, more, or even enough. I was free to BE! Alive with no restraints in His holiness. We are all wired with a lifelong drive to pursue the Freedom Founder and His original fingerprints on our being. This one life exalted up to God, in liberty of living freely under His grace, our authentic beings, to be just that!

I knew we were traveling onward. I needed to give myself permission to move with the momentum. I was the only one holding myself back now. My inner "freedom fighter" needed to put on her armor of aliveness and march forth.

> For, in any true adventure under grace,
> you never travel the same path twice.

Give me your lantern and compass, give me a map, So I can find my way to the sacred mountain, to the place of Your Presence. —Psalm 43:3 (MSG)

Traveling Upward and Onward

The Rewarder Himself became my greatest traveling companion. I needed to make the migration from my old, fabricated, sinful self to a closer image of His original design. At times, I felt the epic battle, but in other moments, I was totally unaware of His spirit-work. Each layer of uncovering proved to reflect another ladder of Christ's character. Now, in the afterglow, I can see how merciful and ample His rewards truly were in this most precipitous, upward trek. For stripping a soul wide open to allow the transplant of true self is never quick, orderly, or marked with ease. But then, transformative work never is. I needed to face myself, naked in my soul, like I've never before undressed. I had many, many miles of muck and mire to travel through. I needed to be brutally honest with what kept me covered. For my kept coverings was what created the distance, preventing me from forging through on His provision of dry soil in a parted sea. A steep path awaited, with many twists and hairpin turns. No A to Z straight lines here. That's not how soul work works.

The life-sustaining decision to let go became the greatest of ascents. For once the cocoon is spun, there is no turning back. It becomes a spiritual dance between what was and what is to be. It is an internal journey toward the light, a journey not for the self-directed but for the yielded in spirit. It was far from any futile former path. My call was simply to follow the Way Maker, but following Him was a must, for to stay the same would have disgraced and grieved the very heart of my Lord Jesus. He loves this girl, even within the ugliness of her human sin nature. And His love always proves worthy. I felt charged to keep pace with the Path Giver. "Righteousness will go before Him and shall make His footsteps our pathway" (Psalm 85:13). I didn't want to inhale a single breath of air without His spirit close to mine. I no longer could depend on myself (a growing godsend), as it was adequately an aid in making me more pliable to mold and trainable toward His trust. I needed to trust Him to grant the placement of each step. "Since we live by the Spirit, let us keep in step with the Spirit" (Galatians 5:25). I needed to actually climb and conquer the peak of the mountain I had previously only wandered around.

Together, we walked the wilderness paths. Whenever the terrain dramatically changed, I found myself trying to analyze or judge the road by how it felt or how it looked to me. I named the road through my feelings—Rocky, Winding, Stable, or Treacherous. But it's different in the Holy Land. The most famous roads in Zion are not named for what they feel like nor for their condition. Instead, they have names like the Road to Bethlehem, the Damascus Road, the Emmaus Road, and the Jericho Road. These famous roads were named for places, not just places but destinations. Their names come from where they took them. I was learning not to judge the condition of the road or how it made me feel. I needed to keep my eye on the Trusty Terrain Guide and go where He was taking me.

He would manifest His presence when needed (Exodus 13:22). For never does He remove the cloud by day or the pillar of fire by night from its place in front of us. His choice is never to leave us orphaned. It is the intention of His heart to follow closely. His presence is what propels the forward movement.

Over and again, I found the Spirit Keeper proving Himself faithful. If I lagged behind, my flesh became fearful, questioning if His footprints had turned cold. Oh, how foolish of me! Never once did He gauge a step so wide that I could not follow. His nature of immeasurable love would never allow such an action. The Great Shepherd measured each step to personally fit the ability of this one lost wandering lamb. He remained close. Even when I didn't feel Him, I somehow knew His eye was on me. He revealed Himself to me as I prayed, "My Lord, keep the eye of my spirit ever upon Yours, the window of my soul surrendered toward Thee." The Path Giver is always enlivened by prayer.

He never wanted me to take control or feel compelled to force the path. So I often found myself needing to re-surrender. And in my weaker moments, when I needed a more tangible touch of truth, He provided earthly angels at just the anointed times on my voyage. I needed a few close ones to see the evolution of myself through their eyes. And filled with thanksgiving, I'm beyond grateful for each of you. I know you know who you are, for you journeyed with me. You are the ones who stayed. I would most graciously pen your names, but I know it would cause you to blush, for your hearts of humility are sold out to our Father as the Founder of All Good and Godly. And those of you who came for a briefer encounter with your wisdom and healing were His unlikely and most appreciated angels in disguise. Each believing what I couldn't yet see. I love you all, my godly ones!

> True friends are angels who lift us to our feet when our wings have trouble remembering how to fly.

The time was present to forge onward and upward, for a work that the generations that traveled before may not have been able to complete. And out of sincere love, respect, and honor for my great grandparents, their parents, and my own beloved, I longed to march on with what they had spiritually started. The breaking away of generational sin became a responsible position with the Chain Breaker. Ancient ruins, neglected and saved for a more convenient time, could be held no longer in their own confines. The wastelands needed to be revisited, dealt with, and demolished. For when we break chains, our children and their children's children hear their rattlings of redemption too! Possibly the sweetest of earthly sounds. I can only imagine how it is received and heard in the heavenlies. A metamorphosis of soul is *never* just for self. Soul work is legacy work! Although this was a steeper, more strenuous climb than I had experienced before, I knew a royal road of redemption waited for ALL in its path.

> For legacy-work constitutes
> an inexpressibly endless value.

And investments placed in our own bloodlines bring rich dividends.

Then you can tell the next generation detail by detail the story of God.
—Psalm 48:13 (MSG)

Trust me, I would never have chosen the length or depth of this journey. He knew I would not have continued on the path if I had known in advance the mileage my heart-spirit would need to tread. Oh Lord, I praise You for your protective and merciful wisdom, sparing me from such knowledge. You've raised me up through my own personal wilderness to have a newfound respect for the Israelites and their forty-year journey out of exile. No matter how long you travel, you will birth what needs to come forth at its destined time, never leaving a willing heart to remain as is. This very truth has become my glory song.

> I'm thanking you God, from a full heart,
> I'm writing the book on your wonders.
> I'm whistling, laughing, and jumping for joy;
> I'm singing your song, High God.
> —Psalm 9:1 (MSG)

All Christ-engaged travels are refined and completed in their perfected times, but never in finality until our heavenly homecomings. It is a glory-to-glory sanctification of manner. And we are still en route, adding a bit more color and character to the wings as we enter the chrysalis and allow yet another spin. I find myself awed with a new level of adoration, as I am shown another similarity through the lens of the majestic Monarch. For it is the only insect to migrate up to 3,500 miles. Such an amazing feat for these most delicate ones; the longest trek of all insects! And only the fourth generation of monarchs successfully completes this lengthy journey, for the first three generations will die within six weeks after escaping from their cocoon husks during their migration south.

I am moved with tears of exaltation as I write, for His grace is grandiose! He longs for each of us to be fourth-generation butterflies! He pines for our wings to make the 3,500-mile soul trek for His glory and for our generational ancestors and the future generations yet to be. I am speechless (something rarely seen), for my heart sees how truly far His love reaches, deep into the crevices of the most broken and underdeveloped spaces of a soul. Beloved Lord, You are my sustaining milkweed. Just as You are the host plant to the Monarch, Your nectar sweeter than any other. You loved and cared for me when I could not love or care for myself. You carried me in the impressions of your holy footprints, gracing me as I slipped into your sacred sandals when I no longer could stand. Each step was purposefully planned, never once leaving, growing weary, or ceasing to grace. Never once. And in all my times of exasperation, falling backwards, and failing forward, and still not fully seeing my identity through your eyes, you never grew tired or stopped walking with me. Instead, You held me. You held me up, held me upright, held me upright in Your arms. Just like the cremaster of the chrysalis.

You were the anchor that held my soul.

Father God, the gate is narrow and few will choose it (Matthew 7:14). Help us be courageous ones. Place a burning fire deep within to follow where You choose us to fly. All we need for this journey is life's ultimate road map and its close traveling companion; the Holy Word and its most Supreme Author. Map and Guide will maneuver us through. For both are *living!* May You find us treating them as such, fully Alive! (Hebrews 4:12).

My Beloved Sacred Soul Maker,

Help me to pass through on dry land. Let me not camp in the plain but give me the mountain. Although some youth was spent in the wilderness, let my strength be renewed by the energy of Your Holy Spirit. For the kingdom and the King live within.

Come. Come and carry us through a journey of Your making for the Master's use. Don't leave us where we are. Move us. Move us to more. Move us to become … Authentically ALIVE in Christ!

Section II

The Inner Line
to
the Transformative Touch

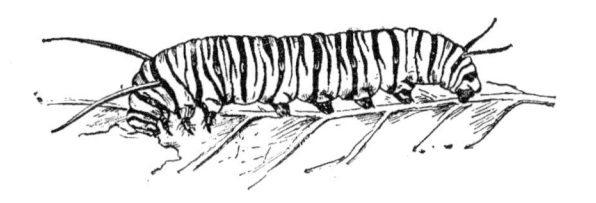

When One is pretending, the entire body revolts. —Anais Nin

Then I acknowledged my sin to you and did not cover up my iniquity.
—Psalm 32:5 (NIV)

Chapter 2

Covered and Attempting Flight

Let's start our migration toward freedom. But to fly authentically free, we must look at the coverings. For it is the coverings that keep our wings stationary, unsuitable for flight.

What images come to mind when you hear the word *covered*? Freshly fallen snow blanketing the majestic Colorado Rocky Mountains? An endless field of bold, brightly golden sunflowers immersing a Dakotan prairie? Or an invaluable heirloom quilt resting on top of a bed? Or perhaps your mind goes to a common phrase used for support and prayer over a loved one—"I've got you covered." In all statements, the term represents a most positive visage; assuring beauty, love-roots, encouragement, and life-gracing aid.

But there is another kind of covering that doesn't serve us as faithfully. In fact, it is drastically detrimental and a great destroyer to our faith walks. And the unfortunate reality is that not a single one of us is exempt from or can escape its wrath. We simply become candidates for coverings just by being born outside the Garden walls. Outside—in fallen heritage, where the graceless impersonation of oneself sets up stage.

Crafting an unwise choice: To Cover.

Graceless and Grounded

I still remember what I was wearing, for the day left an imprint of such unworthiness. Although a half-century has past and being a mere child in the sixth year of my life, I began the day with an innocence and naivete, much like any first-grade child should. I was dressed in my snappy plaid skirt with a collared short-sleeve shirt tucked into the wide elastic waistband. I was sporting my stylish black-and-white saddle shoes with white ankle socks. And adorning my attire was a colorful spirit of aliveness, with just a smidgen of attitude. I loved school and being with classmates. I couldn't articulate such things at the time, but I can give them their voice now. For something happened on this ruinous day that I couldn't give effective utterance or understanding to until decades later. Something knavish took place inside my small blossoming soul. Something was being stolen. An arrow was shot through to disrupt the trust of my purer identity.

The enemy aspires to shoot arrows of unworthiness smack dab into the core of identity and giftedness. He prefers not to bother with lesser targets. Taking down and destroying divinity is always his perfected aim. Although enemy arrows strike in varied ways, they carry a common theme; to take out the worth and value of our soul divinity. And on this very day, my innocence and identity were being targeted.

With the bow drawn, the arrow flew.

Hitting a bull's-eye dead on into my worthiness.

Scoring a covering

right where divinity lived.

I was simply encouraging a young classmate whose desk was beside mine. I liked the colors she was using on her drawing and wanted to let her know. Immediately following my intended compliment of kindness, my first-grade teacher called out my name and asked me to come to the front of the classroom. With eager anticipation of being the chosen one, my blonde ponytail swayed from side to side, as I left my desk and walked forward, never imaging that her heart-intent would be mega-miles from mine. As I approached the teacher, her words *STRUCK*. They severed, stung, piercing deep to my core worth. The arrow had hit. Its damage began bleeding throughout. In a dual cord of confusion and disbelief, she told me to lie down on the cold tile flooring in front of the entire classroom for speaking out of turn. I obediently did as I was told and remained there for the completion of the school day. I can't share my ill-stunned thoughts, for I don't believe I could process whatever they may have been. I'm certain feelings of utter confusion, shame, and ridicule were more than my underdeveloped mind of six years could accurately account for.

But I did make one unfortunate assessment through the midst of this incident. I made a vow, a vow based on faulty trust. Through my feeble attempt to make some sort of sense out of the situation, I vowed I would never be in such a predicament again. Whatever it would take, I would suppress a portion of myself to become a more acceptable me. I was now under the influence of the arrow and seeing a need to trust in the fabrication of myself. I was making myself somewhat dependent now on who I thought I was going to need to be. I would need to please, for being myself got me in trouble. I didn't do it right. I wasn't quite right. I was made wrong. It felt faulty to be me.

After the class was dismissed, I was excused off the floor. I went to retrieve the only garment still to be found in the coatroom. There on its hook was my fluffy button-down cream sweater. As I reached for its comfort, I knew it was no longer just for warmth.

I was going to use it from this day forward to

COVER myself with.

You see, from birth, we are all graced with divinity. If you ever want to know your spiritual giftings, just listen to the stories of your youth spoken back to you. Your actions through the tales are often from a more authentic self. They give a bend toward originality. And I remember what was shared over me. I was the only one, out of the four children in our family, to stand up in my stroller to wave and greet strangers passing by. Their existence mattered. Greatly. I needed to address them with extending a gift of exhortation through a joyful smile and a worthy wave of recognition. And still to this day, I place great value on another's existence. For really, what trumps relationship in this earthly realm? I even prefer to know the waiters and waitresses in a restaurant on a first name basis before I let their servant's heart bless mine. It could be why coaching, hospitality, and teaching are dutiful loves. They involve noticing and encouraging the light in others. I love to see the goodness in another and express what is so readily apparent back to them.

Our biblical King David is known to have been a renaissance man; a musician, warrior, and poet. But I aspire to what was David's greatest gift. Identifying giftedness and greatness in others. Lord, train our eyes and ears to see and hear that which holds Your beauty. In the broken, the unfortunates, the blessed, and the needy; in all. Help us recognize the You that is in another. And in unison, sister sojourner, we say, Amen!

I have written this reminder on the inside cover of my current gratitude journal:

Be a God-Noticer!

In EVERY situation,

In EVERY interaction,

In EVERY day—

Be a Noticer of the Good.

Each of you have original bends that are just yours!

And a very brief but beneficial sidenote nugget (or a bunny trail, however you choose to view this.)

Here's a free test to determine your spiritual gifts, which you can take at your leisure. Be taken away with what you are already bestowed with. You may want to take one (or both) of the following spiritual gifts assessments and then summarize your results:

www.cpcsda.org/uploads/Spiritual-Gifts-Inventory.pdf

exchristian.net/images//wagner_modified_houts.pdf

Momentarily, pause before the Mighty Weaver and ponder the works on your wings. Write them out. Keep them close. Reflect on your spiritual gifts with the Loving Master. Live them as a glory song, for they are the gifts you give back to the Great Giver.

But unfortunately, infiltrating through our graced giftedness, we are subject to attack. I have grown to see the mercilessness of the enemy through spiritual gifting, attacking our very identity. Satan's position is to undermine identities. He even tried with Jesus Himself. While Jesus was in the wilderness for forty days and nights, Satan presented Christ with three temptations: ordering Christ to turn stones into bread, jump off the temple, and win the kingdoms of the world through false worship. But before the devil's insidious promptings even began, he first desired for Christ to *question* His identity by using a simple, two-lettered word. IF. Matthew 4:3 begins, "If you are the Son of God ..." A calculated strike against Christ's identity was being falsely declared with that single word. The enemy has a very subtle weapon that he uses to make you doubt and defuse your worth. Is God for real, and is your identity found in Him? Merely having us question—

Who is God?

And

Who am I?

Most of us live our entire lives as strangers to ourselves. We know more about others than we know about ourselves. Our true identities get buried beneath the mistakes we've made, the insecurities we've acquired, and the lies we've believed. We're held captive by others' expectations. We're uncomfortable in our own skin. And we spend far too much emotional, relational, and spiritual energy trying to be who we're not.
—Mark Batterson

British preacher G. Campbell Morgan summarized our present

moment well, even from his early twentieth-century vantage point, by noting that when people lose their consciousness of God, they do not lose the sense of their need for God. They simply substitute the false for the true.

> These two questions—who are You, Lord? And who am I?—are imperative in the divine quest toward intimacy with God. —Beth Moore, *The Quest*

The way we see God profoundly shapes who we are. The way we view God, ourselves, the world, and the future determines our outlook, moods, morals, relationships, and experiences. It's vital to pay attention to how we see Him, for our level of intimacy with God is also based on what we believe about ourselves. Authentic intimacy requires the quest for knowing both identities—God and self.

This connection or lack of it directs the entire course of our life.

> What comes into our minds when we think of God is the most important thing about us. —A.W. Tozer

Satan's strategy hasn't changed from our Garden-of-Eden ancestors. He wants us to misunderstand God, doubt His Word and character, in hopes of keeping us in constant confusion in terms of who we are.

> We labor increasingly to preserve an imaginary existence and neglect the real. —Blaise Pascal

> They sewed fig leaves together as makeshift clothes for themselves. —Genesis 3:7 (MSG)

Fig-Leaf Garments

The damage begins unsuspectedly, without warning. And the aftermath of the arrow is rarely recognized. It strikes at the age of innocence, before we are even equipped with proper tools for battle. Although its affects may seem trivial, the denied devastation, if not dealt with, leaks destruction. Arrows sneak in and strike, cursing us to cover. In my inadequate, youth-filled belief system, I somehow, someway felt I wasn't okay. I thought I needed to now change or control something. And any form of what we imagine we can manage is merely creating an illusion all its own.

A false sense of self-dependence was being birthed. I believed that somehow now, I had to be careful to be a more "acceptable" me. I had to please, perform, and try to appear good, believing the real me wasn't created quite right. I felt a need to cover and hide what wasn't approved of. But in any hiddenness, the arrow only continues to wound, leaving promised healing—unhealed. As I write, I am being shown such similarity from the first of our ancestors. The apple didn't fall far from the Tree of Life. The apple never falls far for any of us. Was I really any different? Just like my originated bloodline, I was feeding on fruit of faulty wisdom.

Precisely like our ancestors Adam and Eve did.

And the questions swirl: How did my coverings originate? Where did I find my coverings? How did I become covered? What even are my coverings? How do I break free from my own coverings?

To imply greater understanding, let's begin where it all began—

In the Garden.

You know the story. In the beginning was God's garden of grandeur, Paradise. Adam and Eve walked among this perfected existence one-in-spirit with Supreme Father God. But in this place of serene tranquility, where the nakedness of body and soul wore no shame, a series of tragic events took place that caused every human being to falter from their designed destiny. Not only from the apple-biting act of original sin, but also from the *covering* of it. God generously gave Adam and Eve the privilege of all the abundant fruits from the trees, with only one restriction— "Do not eat from the tree of the knowledge of good and evil, for if you do, you will die." But the slimy serpent tempted their fleshly desires, which trumped their obedience, and they ate.

A sidenote nugget on the matter of obedience: Our fleshly desires, still to this day, can want to trump obedience. Oh, the lessons in obedience I continue to learn from my own self-will and stubbornness. And a nugget of truth that I limped away with many years ago is this—Obedience is *serious business* to God. When He sets healthy boundaries, we can trust it is always for our betterment through His best resolute. His Holy Word confirms, "My dear child, don't shrug off God's discipline, but don't be crushed by it either. It's the child He loves that he disciplines; the child He embraces, He also corrects" (Hebrews 12:7–8 MSG). I've had several tough lessons of correction through the years. I specifically remember the time I clearly heard in my heart, "Leave well enough alone." Those were His earmark words. But I pushed past the boundary line, taking just a teeny toe-length bit beyond, placing me in a disobedient district of spirit. And I paid a consequence of correction I dearly needed to learn. We can choose the pain of discipline or the pain of disappointment. We can bend in submission or break in rebellion. Again, obedience is serious business (John 14:21).

And back to the Garden we go.

After eating the forbidden fruit, Adam and Eve's eyes were opened to see themselves. They now connected themselves to their newly ingested fruit, the knowledge of self-independence. They not only walked away from the tree, they walked away from their True Source of Life. God's breath no longer flowed as their entire sustaining force. They still breathed and had a pulse, but their authentic aliveness of divine identity was already in decay. From this day forward, they had to live with not the solitary knowing of A Person but knowing rules and having free reign with self-will. Unfortunately, we find ourselves in this same place today.

> Fallen, fleshly beings.

But I believe what happens next in the story line is even more important. The garden-words of God's love came speaking forth; "Where are you?" Not asking geographically, metaphorically, or even figuratively, asking soulfully. "Where is your soul?" Giving Adam and Eve an opportunity to examine their hearts with the Heart Knower, provoking an opening to address their sin and purge its impurity—"Then I acknowledged my sin to you and did not cover up my iniquity" (Psalm 32:5), allowing us all once again to fully connect with our Creator God. But when they heard the footsteps walking among them, they cowered. They hid. Shame has a way of inducing fear, and its sister action is the frantic flight response to run and hide. And among the knowingness of their shame,

> they sewed fig leaves together and made a *covering* for themselves.

Their chosen actions only making them slave masters to their own self-induced bondage, for instead of being cleansed through repentant hearts with a godly sorrow,

> their fig-leaf garments became even more rancid in nature than the rotting fruit in their stomachs!

And what do we do today with this naked truth?

We do just what Adam and Eve did. We hide our sinful natures and the wounding of enemy arrows.

> We sew fig leaves of fabrication together
>
> and make coverings of falsehood.

We grow afraid to show our real selves. It's a craftiness of the enemy when we hide our glaring imperfections in an effort to hold some vestige of self-esteem and subtle pride. And when we come with a cloak of any kind, it hinders our transparency to willingly lift it up to the light. Whatever is kept hidden and behind closed doors remains buried alive and unrenewable. Often, the truth of the matter feels harder than the lie. We find ourselves believing the same mistruth Adam and Eve did. A devilish, dirty lie. A well-spun lie brought down through the ages. A lie keeping us far from liberation.

The Principle Lie.

And the Principle Lie worms its misbelief.

Hidden coverings will keep us safe.

But may we never forget.

The Principle Lie comes from the Lie-Speaker.

And the Lie-Speaker, LIES!

Terribly uncreative is the evil one. The Primary Lie is still what he leads with today, fooling us into believing our coverings will keep us safe. So our human tendency is to hide versus reveal. We find ourselves covering the memories, the pain, the insecurities, the shame, until we no longer can be honestly known. We can even hide and lose our connection with the Redemptive One and our true self. And we lie loudest when we lie to ourselves. For we are only creating a greater distance to our desired freedom lands. And then we often, unfortunately, choose not to go back to the stuck places and let His radiance redeem. For in the enemy's schemes of trickery, his arrows will remain secure and hidden if we continue to live out the Principle Lie. This keeps us caged from ever wearing our purposed wings, tempting us with whispers that it's better not to be fully known. After all, what will others think of me? When in reality, these slithering's of untruth only enslave, keeping us captive to our coverings. Sadly, we ourselves become the obstacle that keeps us from taking the coverings off. For our coverings need removal for real redemption. But they are our created coverings.

And not only are they that—they are NOT God's. God never intended for us to wear such a weighty burden. We are loved beyond our imaginations and more fully known by Him than we experience in this realm. Coverings are human-made and need to be shed. This is the reason for the sacred shed blood from the Eternal Lamb. And we are all welcome to come. Just as we are. Covered. Even the commonplace coverings every breathing life encounters, begs to break off. Negative thoughts, unbelief, judgment, insecurities, fears, and let us not forget to mention, pride. Pride is the mother lode behind all sin. Pride is the instrument we play when we think we know the tune better than the Great Musician Himself.

Detrimentally, every covering is an unwise choice.

Coverings cripple.

Keeping us far from freedom wings.

> We are a forgetful people. We need storytellers. We need someone to lay the drama of God's love before us. We need to be reminded of the uncommon grace of God.
> —William R. White

Storied

> You become. It takes a long time. That's why it doesn't happen often to people who break easily or have sharp edges or who have to be carefully kept. Generally, by the time you are Real, most of your hair has been loved off and your eyes drop out and you get loose in the joints and very shabby. But these things don't matter at all, because for one you are Real; you can't be ugly, except to people who don't understand.
> —Margery Williams, *The Velveteen Rabbit*

This classic story, written in 1922, continues to be treasured by generations because it expresses truths we know deep down—that love is what makes us real, and that becoming real is worth any amount of pain. I recently read that writers tend to grow up and live out their favorite childhood stories. I'd never put any thought to it before and am not certain about its merit, but I was finding it to prove truthful in my case. I never realized it at the time, but my two favorite books to read to our infant sons (now adult men) had such similar themes. I'll still to date share these stories with adult coaching clients if the shoe fits. The titles were *The Little Rabbit Who Wanted Red Wings* by Carolyn Bailey and Max Lucado's *You Are Special*. These classic stories carry the same theme as my current dabblings—themes of authenticity, of becoming, accepting, and loving your one true self. The moral nugget of the first book is summed up with the truth that if we are spending time trying to be someone else, who is going to be you? And in Max's book, he implies it's not the opinions of the wooden people known as Wemmicks that give one their worth, but our true value comes from Eli, the Great Woodcarver of the wooden people, reminding us how deeply we are loved, just the way we were created to be.

I now see why these two children's books were so significant to read to my sons. I wanted to instill and weave deeply into their lives an area of grayness that needed a purer light in my own. The spiritual journey of becoming real was knocking on my heart long before I saw its path and opened its door. Isn't that just like God, though? To have a mother already longing for her children to possess what her own soul was in greater search of. The music of a truer self was already beginning to play within, and I didn't want to miss out on what the Incomparable Composer was already creating,

my most irresistible adventure of all.

Becoming Real!

We each have a story. Our own story. Ones that begin at the earliest moments of our lives. We create our stories out of necessity. They explain events that may have been traumatic, challenging, or confusing, and we want to put understanding or reason to them. They allow us to hold on to those we love, when they either did not or could not respond to our most essential need to be loved and recognized. But through our life-scripts, God is always on standby. He waits for us to embrace His penmanship, as we allow Him to be the Greatest Written Character. But because we live in a broken Eden, a failed paradise, our stories have misbeliefs woven throughout.

Our stories have limits.

In our youth, we set up stories to live by. But around midlife (maybe this is what a midlife crisis is all about), the storylines and their mistruths begin to crumble. Their structures were never meant to be sturdy for the full length of the journey. An internal quaking arises. Once helpful, they no longer make sense of our world. Now they play their part in the Principle Lie. No longer does the life-song resonate true tones of harmony. And the mind grows weary in playing what the heart can't delete. Costing us distorted vision and hidden authenticity within the woven pages. But we bartered much of our essential self for the false promise the story made.

> To be loved but not known is comforting but superficial. To be known and not loved is our greatest fear. But to be fully known and truly loved is, well, a lot like being loved by God. —Tim Keller

But whatever it takes, dearest sojourner, may we not get stuck in the middle of our stories! We hold the pen in hand to create the next sentence, the following chapter, and a most promised conclusion. When we trust our unknown future to a God we know is authoring each page; our hope in Him is our satisfying end. Even within our taxing plots, filled with impossibility, His heart inclines to edit our storylines with much promise.

> God rewrote the text of my life when I opened the book of my heart to His eyes! —Psalm 18:24 (MSG)

The Great Interpreter and myself began to rewrite. I was finally coauthoring my own life rather than allowing myself to be authored by others.

Yes, in our adulthoods, we are given the awesome opportunity and prized privilege to rewrite our text with the Trusty and True One, with a steadiness and sure-footedness of WHO our identities are now founded on, in, and through.

But working through our stories can be messy. You may want to travel with a counselor, spiritual mentor, or coach, or ask a trusty friend to walk with you. Uncovering coverings can require much weight. Not everyone is chosen or can handle to hear all or will be a good fit. It is a pure privilege to journey in such an intimate special space. Pray for His honorable ones (a bit more on this later).

Our stories offer up hope to another's darkness. Often in our stories, we don't want to relive the hurt or shame, so we remain silent. But we need to be good stewards of our pain. When we share the difficult parts of our story, not only do we find healing, but their resurrected testimony has the power to heal others. We are gifting hope through our tales. Together, we witness the power of redemption and the ways God shows up throughout and within the storylines. Maybe that's the reason I write. Even in the middle of the messiness of my story, it is my story, and journeying with the Script-Revealing Savior gives it full meaning. It restores its merit. Articulating it with Him postures me to hear further hints from the Mightiest Manuscriptor, engraving His excellence deep into the pages of my soul journey. I watch His abilities turn the scars into stars, the messiness into a message, and the trials into testimony. They are stories of redemption; telling about the battles fought, the fears conquered, and the dreams chased. They share about the whole and holy found in the valleys, coming out of the hallow—victorious and healed. Although not every story ends well by earthly standards, each saved life becomes His best seller. When we journey with Him through all the burnt places, in the final chapter, we are promised bouquets of roses instead of ashes (Isaiah 61:3 MSG). All charred soul, made beautiful.

Each one of our stories matters more than we think.

We need to extend our stories to others, so they know they're not alone.

Let's mark the milestones of His mercy and love,

revealing how God rebuilds ancient landmarks.

Throughout the Old Testament, God commands Israel to "remember" by building stone altars proclaiming His provision. He wants us to remember too! To remember who our Redeemer, Healer, Defender, Rescuer, Savior, and King is, and what He is capable of doing in each personal "hall of faith" heart. When we voice what God has done in our lives, we declare WHO He is. No wonder the enemy wants us to live in shame and stay quiet in our stories. Our stories hold healing power. Our stories let us know we never walk alone. Our stories are memorial stones of freedom. Our stories are testaments to His truths and promises. They leave markers of remembrance behind for those who carry the torch well beyond our final inscriptions on the pages of our last chapter.

Processing the journey with the Amazing Author of All Time is what makes this an intimate love story. As we processed the pages, I discovered it was based more on provision, protection, comfort, guidance, promise, and praise hallelujahs; penning together a script of sanctification. I needed to remind myself that each day held a fresh, unmarked page. And TODAY is the first day of the rest of my life. I was writing my story woven into the fabric of the Grand Story. His Book is boss! And to tell my story is to tell of Him. Our stories continue to be written. They remain unfinished. Our stories remain in His authoritative hand. And we have a say, not only in how the Lord and your lovely self will continue transcribing the daily entries, but also in how the lines will translate onward to encourage, impact, and bless others.

Our soul stories are to be shared.

Our own emotional and spiritual stuckness (through coverings) is the slate on which we start to rewrite the script. As our authentic freedom-walks ache to come alive, we feel somewhat powerless to change and yet know we must participate in moving toward the chrysalis of Christ for permanent transformation to take place. The trappings of our preceding story are only a masquerade in a nature of miswritten lines. They now whisper false security; "I'll keep you protected from the pain of abandonment and rejection. I'll keep you safe—hidden, far from being found out." But unfortunately, the coverings only keep us from becoming real and known (and, tragically, they keep us unloved). Without full knowledge, we have subconsciously ingrained both the storylines and its mistruths to fit into a fictional character. We need to drop this "crippling caterpillar syndrome" in our stories and choose the uphill climb to the cremaster, rewriting the storylines with the Greatest Author of All Time.

The One who storied us fully from the womb.

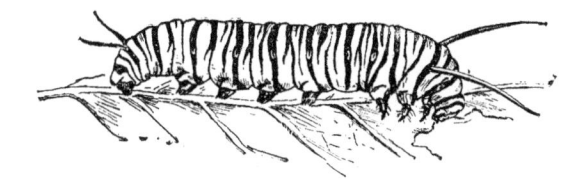

How does one become a butterfly? You must want to fly so much that you are willing to give up being a caterpillar. —Trina Paulus

In the presence of trouble, some people grow wings; others buy crutches. —Harold Ruoff

Crippling Caterpillar Syndrome

It looks as though the crawling caterpillar's entire life revolves around eating, just eating—never satisfied, always looking for more. And heartwrenchingly, some will passively remain on the plant, never choosing to climb upward, simply awaiting death. But the caterpillar is designed for greater aspirations than just feeding off the milkweed and remaining earthbound. Although its stunted legs don't present any promise for flight, it continues to thrive, knowing the enormous importance of being the only catalyst to crawl up the milkweed and form the cremaster. So utterly necessary is the cremaster to the promised formation of the cocoon. For the cremaster is the anchor to its life force for the engagement of future wings! Without this hope, wings would never see the light of day. So the caterpillar continues to munch away on the milkweed, with a more focused intent—to climb. I wish it was like that with all of humankind. That we fully believed in our destiny and let nothing derail our focus, that regardless of the challenges, we too would ache for the uphill climb. But somewhere along the way, using our caterpillar legs as a crutch seems the easier way through, merely surviving for the brief feast on the host plant. And when we indulge too long there, we grow sluggish and eventually form a spiritual retirement stage, allowing preferred coverings to become the crippling crutch. It keeps us from the upward ascent, for we cannot be taught to walk freely when trusting to a crutch.

> And coverings come as diverse as we are individuals.

Let's name just a few of the common false selves: Self-Defeater. Posed Perfectionist. Martyr Mary. People Pleaser. Worrywart. Overachiever. Control Freak. Intimacy Avoider. Pot Stirrer. Internal Condemner. Wall Builder. Prideful Promoter. Grace Denier. Disbeliever. Chaos Creator. Silent Stuffer. Righteous Rebel. Sarcastic Slammer. Pity City Dweller. Boundary Breaker. Envy Indulger. Judgmental Juror. Victim Chooser. And on and on the list goes.

False selves rear their ugly heads through our own self-imposed thoughts and habits. They can be seen through chemical dependency, intellectualism, theological rigidity, food control, augmented personalities, extraneous activities, codependency, and a score of other things. No matter what our coverings may be, in order to recognize and heal from them, we must feel them, admit them, own them, and bring them into the light of Christ.

> False selves only remind us to remain undercover, whispering so suggestively, "It's safer to be superficial."

The Principle Lie is well at work with cunning deceitfulness. It likes to lay silent within a subliminal softness, but powerful in its suggestion. It plots with a slyness of false accusation, staking its claim—I'm not okay the way I am. I'm different. I don't fit in. I am not enough. How will I ever be loved for who I am?" The arrows inject misbeliefs of being unlovable, incapable, undesirable, unforgiveable, unknown, insignificant, sometimes even a mistake. Any covering aims to tear down the transparency of authenticity, leaving us with a need to stitch, repair, and disguise the torn places. And through our attempts to shield and mend, we begin to find ourselves living a syndrome of soul-sickness. We give up on promised wings, keeping ourselves in the crawling caterpillar stage, never advancing onward. An abnormality, now formed through mistaken thinking, keeps us on earth's dirt. We carry along with us a darkened weight from a lack of exposure to the truest light. And the weight of the coverings cripple, making us lame and unable to make the incline forward to form the cremaster and spin the cocoon. This makes the wearing of wings an impossibility. Knowing who God is and finding our true identity under His wing is how we thrive in the sweeter of spots. We often become too preoccupied with what we are not, too busy spawning a more acceptable self. We become more interested in self-preservation than self-forgetfulness. We can't accept who we are. We feel we are not right or not enough. And in all honesty, we never will be, without God. But what then? What happens when our new identity-spirits in Christ just don't seem to kick in? Why are we for some reason still not walking in the reality of transformed redemption?

These questions bring to mind the parable of the four soils talked about in the Harvest Story in Matthew 13. The farmer sowed good seed, but not all the seed sprouted. Some seed fell on rocky soil, withered, and died quickly. And some was strangled out by the weeds. Other seed never even took root. And the surviving soul plants that grew had varying yields of produce. But seed that fell on good earth produced a harvest beyond the wildest of dreams.

> God tills barren ground for good seed.

The seed cast on good earth is the person who really hears the truths of God and takes them to heart, fully believing! Belief cannot be forced to follow a mathematical formula or our own self-propelled plans. Rather, it is the miracle work of God's Holy Spirit as He grows us to believe in His words and truths, preparing the pathway to experience His presence. So when we give energy and power to the whispered lies or to an empty well, we are like withered seed constructing the counterfeit. Planting seed in infertile ground produces fruitlessness. Stunting our growth in the doughtiness of disbelief, makes us victims who don't believe that our true spirit flights even exist. It keeps us slumberous once again; believing the Principle Lie over God's timeless truth.

> This causes our internal tune to sound more like a broken record than mystifying music,
>
> like an instrument with distorted or broken strings.

And unfortunately, our inner peace and harmony begin to play tunes of discord as the authentic soul begins to drift to a song it was never intended to sing. We no longer feel secure to beat from our own exclusive drum alongside the Master Conductor. We choose to change up the lyrics and compose a different melody. Our fabricated, rehearsed rhythm pulling us further away from our original position on God's dance floor of life. Leaving us no longer in step with the Leading Prince's melodic tune, as we leave behind the Original Songwriter's unique notes and their rhythmic timing over us. All sadly unsung.

And when the music fades,
we begin to fabricate.

As we

- barricade
- medicate
- isolate
- eliminate
- compulsively generate
- minimalize
- rationalize
- compromise
- idolize

Anything to keep the lie quiet, at bay, and behaving itself.

I will give you the keys of the kingdom of heaven; whatever you bind on earth will be bound in heaven, and whatever you loose on earth will be loosed in heaven. —Matthew 16:19 (NIV)

For everyone who asks receives; he who seeks finds; and to him who knocks, the door will be opened.
—Matthew 7:8 (NIV)

The Master Locksmith

Christ comes via the very citadel of a soul. He knows the inner sanctums and depths that have yet to be plumbed. We all have rooms with shadowing, not necessarily dark because of sin but gloomed because they have been kept closed with coverings. They are the spaces were the false self lives.

Thomas Merton clearly puts his finger on the false self; "This false exterior, superficial, social self is made up of prejudices, whimsy, posturing, pharisaic self-concern and pseudo dedication. The false self is a human construct built by selfishness and flights from reality. Because it is not the whole truth of us, it is not of God. And because it is not of God, our false self is substantially empty and incapable of experiencing the love and freedom of God."

Graciously, no door is too difficult to open for the Master Locksmith. God knows precisely how to woo each soul. So we hand over the keys, crying forth to come and break the code of our covered hearts. God knows how to cut off our coverings, because nothing liberates quite like love.

I was longing for the Love Lavisher to reconnect my spirit to something—anything—closer to who I was meant to be. He began showing me something very significant beyond the caterpillar crawl. An assured belief of forming wings was being discovered through a more transparent flare of myself, as I gazed on Him, creating a view just limpid enough to begin to trust the transformation. A beauty was being birthed through acceptance, a self-acceptance of being content in my starting place. For I knew God owned the ultimate key of love. Only His indescribable essence can bear full ownership to such a worthy entrance to my bolted-in bondage. And He is amazingly efficient in cracking the code and deciphering all that needs to be dispelled. Even if I didn't understand His process of unlocking, I was okay with that. I didn't need to know. The key was never mine to manage. I just kept asking, seeking, and knocking. I knew He had opened the door, holding it ajar, giving me clearance to open myself up more fully. And I could hear His love-words through the crack in the opening, "Come out of hiding; you're safe here with Me." It's in His guaranteed caretaking countenance, that whoever knocks—the door will be opened onto him.

Unlatch us, Lord.

I knew I was safe to access any chamber of my being with Christ. He is always the safe place to fall. And He will call community alongside to help with the healing work how He deems. He brings them, the necessary ones. It amazes me the few select that were brought into my life. I could never have picked them like He did. They were further along on their journey than I. They held more experience, more wisdom, more freedom, more faith, more understanding, more of His love. And we do become more like the God "our people" spend time with. Iron sharpens iron. I ached to grow spiritually and wanted to surround myself with such substantial women and men. He so lovingly provided my perfect fits.

The next best thing to being wise oneself is to live in a circle of those who are. —C. S. Lewis

Permanent healing-work calls for community. And I was blessed with a beautiful and bountiful array—a queen of generativity, a co-heart, a soul sister (and my biological one too), an island princess, a wellness doc, a prayer walking partner, an alternative wellness advocate, and my husband, family, and friends who saw the better half of my true self before she was more fully birthed. They came when I needed them. Not all at once and over a decade and more of time. But each in their perfected time and designated ways.

Words of gratitude I speak over each of you—

Every time you cross my mind, I break out in exclamation of thanks to God. —Philippians 1:3 (MSG)

And these God-chosen lives all around—what splendid friends they make. —Psalm 16:3 (MSG)

But may I add, be discerning with who will hold you with holy care. Pray for wisdom to know who the ones are assigned to help the Master Locksmith unlock. This rite to journey close beside you must be earned. Bible scholar Beth Moore teaches in her *Sacred Secrets* study something that has stuck to my inner ribs—Be authentic with all, transparent with most, intimate with few (and, may I add, completely uncovered before Christ). Be prayerful as God provides His desired chosen ones for you to evolve with. A safety net of security must be established, first and foremost. Not all will be safe. Not all will hold it with a tender holiness or a sincere care. Some just want in and may push a bit too forcefully. Others may seek their own agenda. Some will be jealous. Some will be too preoccupied to be present. Or some may even use your intimate trust against you. Oh, but the wonders of being on a breaking-free journey with another! Not much surpasses the beautiful union of discovery, understanding, and celebration shared. There is no friendship quite like it. So seek wise counsel if you feel led. It's biblical to do so, as you choose with discernment and prayer.

Confidently and carefully, the good seed was being tilled into my barren brokenness and tenderly transplanted. So graciously, God chose the perfected field-hands to help me wilt the weeds and replant. I was zealous to be a first of fields in need of harvesting. Our first task is always ourselves. The weeding, the digging deeper, the planting, the pruning—the glorious becoming fruit. Oh yes, the bearing of fruit.

We never labor in vain,

as long as we don't lose glimpse of

the Master Gardener.

The Giver of all new seed

growing an abundant harvest!

When we curate masks to be someone else, we vacate our own soul, who has no one else. —Ann Voskamp

❧

Sowing My Soul

The deeper my intimacy roots grew, the more my false self was shown. An awakening to more of a realness, trueness, and trust was being experienced. I wanted to continue morphing but prayed for the process to be gentle. I was as fragile as any newborn wing. My performance was finished. It was time to unmask, time to disrobe. It was time to ditch the worthless wardrobe and get all new duds. Any covering needed to uncloak. My fear of rejection from others or myself needed to unveil. It was time to divulge to the Divine, to take off the costume and rest in His righteousness. The Principle Lie had lied to me long enough.

I screamed back at the Lie Speaker, "Unacceptable! I will not remain as is!"

I will not live here—simply crawling along—getting by. Yet, was I audacious enough to usher in the work to uncover?! The lies will speak again, trying to secure a barrier of failure toward our upward climb. Even just two shady words, from the Lie-Speaker's language, can put a halt to our tracks. The two measly words simply slithering, "It will be too much." Too much work may be involved, too much time has passed, too much has happened to believe in more, too much time out of my schedule, too much apathy, too much history, too much to forgive, too much self-denial, too much water under the bridge, too much anger and bitterness, too much to uncover, too much fear, too much pride; just waaaaay too, too much.

Oh, but my heart pulsed stronger still to the ache of 2 Corinthians 4:1 (MSG):

"We refuse to wear masks and play games. We don't maneuver and manipulate behind the scenes. And we don't twist God's Word to suit ourselves. Rather, we keep everything we do and say out in the open, the whole truth on display, so that those who want to can see and judge for themselves in the presence of God."

I needed a soul-examination in the light of His Presence and Word.

Examine me God, from head to foot, order your battery of tests. Make sure I'm fit inside and out so I never lose sight of your love. —Psalm 139:23–24 (MSG)

Even though He knows what will be found, we still need to usher God in, asking Him to soul-examine us as to what will stay and what needs to go. Embracing the Heart Examiner allows us to see what is holding us back. Change is scary. We may find ourselves wanting to protect our "Don't rock the boat" mentality, pretending things are just fine the way they are. Why stir up any settled dust? Or if I turn on the faucet to inner truth, could I possibly drown from the force of the pressure that held it artificially secured for such a long time? Humanly and honestly, we just want to sweep the painful stuff under the rug. Out of sight—out of mind. But also, unhealed. When we cover, we are only creating expanse between the Heart Examiner and our hearts. And when we hide from the sincerity of this solo relationship, we also remove the intimacy and all that is so beautifully blessed in and through it. Our connection with the Heart Knower is the escape exit out of Egypt. However He chooses to provide the passage way through.

My coverings that were sheathed in the shadowlands, were coming into a greater light under His soul exploration. I found myself believing in the open sky of a new day.

The Soul Maker spoke; "Oh precious one—there's *more* for you.

And His truths were sowing STRONGER than the lies.

Planting firmly into my soul soil.

Disclosure grows deliverance!

I needed to come out of hiding and uncover my authentic me.

I knew One safe enough to start with,

for if I couldn't unveil before the King,

wherever else would I?

When you have to make a choice and don't make it, that is in itself a choice. —William James

For human beings, the whole possibility of redemption lies in their ability to choose to change. —A. W. Tozer

Nothing in all creation is hidden from God's sight. Everything is *uncovered* and laid bare before the eyes of him to whom we must give account.
—Hebrews 4:12–13 (NIV, emphasis mine)

CHAPTER 3

Choosing to Uncover

Just like the fuzzy full-legged caterpillar needs to shed its skin to rise to greater heights, I needed to strip off my graveclothes too. My apparel no longer fit a new, growing expression of ordained beautifulness. I was recognizing that the removal of my former self became the choice. For the fortresses, behind which any ego or stronghold hides, never wants to be torn down or even exposed. It takes courage to become who we really are.

Courage is grace under pressure. —Ernest Hemingway

For it can feel at first like a violent assault on what already is. More like a threat to harm than an action to help. For the imposter self wants to feel safe by continuing to pretend, but the true heart inside bleeds to be more fully known.

That is why it is so hard to choose the change.

It involves an unraveling of the dated threads, allowing the Great Weaver control of the spinning wheel.

A life-altering choice awaited. I was learning how immeasurably powerful choices are. I was understanding the power in our free wills and how vital our will is to transforming work. Free will is the only one thing given to all humankind. The choice is to choose, and our choices matter. Our choices are the sum of our current life. Everything in our lives is a reflection of our choices. If we want different results, we need to make different choices.

And heaven forbid, even in the most tragic of circumstances, we still are graced with the choice of how we will respond. I've seen time and again too many heroic ones who inspire me. On days when I feel like the hill is too hard to climb, I often think of Nick Vujicic and how he was born with no limbs. No arms or legs. Married with children, it is beyond belief what he is doing to glorify God's kingdom work today. He made a choice not to let his circumstance of being born limbless have any negative claim over his life. Certainly, not an attitude for the frail in heart or the faint in faith.

We are bombarded every day with endless decisions and choices, choices on all realms and in all stages of our lives. From the mundane choices of what I will wear or eat for breakfast to the life-altering decisions of what treatment I should pursue for a serious illness or where my life purpose is being most fully utilized and how I will spend my time, energy, and witness. Whether small or large, power of choice is continually active and at work.

> Decision determines Destiny.

Joseph Epstein once said, "We do not choose to be born. We do not choose our parents, or the country of our birth. We do not, most of us, choose to die; nor do we choose the time and conditions of our death. But within this realm of choicelessness, we do choose how we live."

Choice is forever present, directing the course of potential wings. We can choose to remain covered or choose to uncover. But remaining indecisive chokes out growth. Indecision makes us unstable. The beige world of being lukewarm, medium, unsure, and uncommitted paralyzes the flow of faith. The choice of our course is ours. Unfortunately, few will choose the road less traveled. For that means moving beyond comfort zones.

> And we all know how comfortable
> comfort zones can be.

You can't fake authentic surrender for it is the moment you unclench your hands, accept what is, and finally let go to the fertile space provided for divine intervention and unimaginable possibilities. —Kristen Jongen

Life begins at the end of your comfort zone. —Neale Donald Walsh

Uncomfortably Clenched

We can't settle for safe. Constricted within chains that clench us down. I think of the following analogy, as it vividly displays how comfort zones originate and hold us back. I hope this word picture illustrates it to you, as well.

An African baby elephant weighs roughly two hundred pounds and stands about three feet tall at birth. Elephants are often trained in captivity from a very young age of six months or so, by being chained or tied to a stake that is pounded deep into the earth. Longing for its natural instinct to roam, the baby elephant tries to tug and tug on the chain, in hopes of pulling up the stake. It is obvious to everyone except the baby elephant that this stake will soon be unable to hold the elephant in place as its strength grows. But clueless to this capability, the elephant ventures only as far as his chain allows. His circle of captivity is unknowingly being formed. After a number of days or perhaps weeks, the baby elephant will give up. And somberly, the elephant not only gives up; he has now been rewired to believe he will never be able to pull the stake up out of the ground. Despite the fact that within a year's time, he could very easily rip out the stake. Only now, the elephant's lack of belief in his ability to do so has altered the course of his destiny. Even when the animal is released from the stake and his chain is freed, the elephant will choose captivity. The poor creature will never venture out of the circle of the length of its original chain. Now chainless, the baby elephant chooses to stay in its known comfort zone.

Do we unconsciously do the same?

When we quit seeking the deep matters of our heart with God or stop pressing past our comfort plateaus; are we also choosing confinement over breaking free? For it takes energy, submission, resources, and time. It may even shake up our circles of life as we know them to be. But like the baby elephant stuck in its cycle, even when unshackled from its stake, we also can be stuck, living within a cyclical state, lacking forward momentum. We can become like the elephant that wraps its trunk around another elephant's tail and marches in endless, meaningless, captive circles.

How often are our chains loosed and we alone are the obstacle keeping ourselves imprisoned?

Lord, please help us be encouraged to leave our comfort zones and uncover. And help us to encourage others to do the same. We have grown so fearful of being politically correct that we're not even being real with one another. We prefer to stay silent versus being advocates for each other's strength. May we be found encouraging each other to risk unclenching and venture into the unimaginable possibilities.

Otherwise, when we fail to recognize, acknowledge, or uncover the chains of constraint; we too will be held captive, remaining in close quarters, tight circles, comfort zones. We're no different from an elephant's blindness toward his power within.

Lord, shake us free from our earth-shackles.

Loosen us, Lord!

Remove whatever keeps us less connected to You.

Uncovering is foremost a choice, a life call to choose the transition of chain-breaking. It's a tug of internal wars. A tug between the dark and the light, the clinging and the letting go, and the known and the unknown. Ultimately, it's a choice between captivity and freedom. The good news is, we get to choose.

Choose wisely.

> The most important story we will ever write in life is our own—not with ink, but with our choices.
> —Richard Evans

We get to choose to waver any uncertainty toward our freefall. To discharge the unsteadiness in the dropping of the crutches, to move into the abyss without controlling the outcome, to unclench the confining chains.

My choice was made.

And I needed only one thing to coax my crawl upward—

A Secure Connection.

But if you forget about yourself and look to me, you'll find both yourself and me. —Matthew 10:39 (MSG)

The Holy Holder

Uncovering is ineffective without connection. If words such as *stuck, blocked, trapped, frustrated,* or *dissatisfied* resonate within, they are beckoning you to attach and make changes. If our strongholds continue to remain active, if the shadows of past sorrows never cease, or the self-condemnation of our identities never lift, we are not living in authentic aliveness. We are living disconnected from His Crucifixion cause found within His Calvary love.

And this may be the most grievous of all injustices.

Just like the caterpillar needs to climb to form its hook-like anchor (known as the cremaster) for its survival, I knew I was hardwired to do the same. The cremaster threads the provision for the anchored point. It is where the caterpillar attaches and lives before it spins its cocoon. It attaches its spiny, silky little protuberance at the end of its abdomen, like a Velcro button, allowing an unbreakable hold that will support the soon-to-be spinner.

I knew if I wanted to manifest His presence of transformation, I needed to position myself to receive it. I needed to latch into the strongest anchor of all. Christ's holy hook became my cremaster, for He is the direct and only source of living and eternal life. We have an empty void that can only be filled as we are loved and connected with our Cremaster Creator. We need to attach to the strongest of connections before we can bravely enter in.

When you choose to climb, the positioning needed to uncover will present itself. Uncovering is possibly the most brazen act you can do. It's the surrender stage, where you choose trusting over trying. It's the shift in your scale that speaks, "I'm finished working in my own foolish frenzy, striving to produce, and living from exhausting self-efforts." It's the definitive point of no return to the leeks and garlic of Egypt. It's in this decisive moment we confirm to climb, knowing we hold a responsibility to creating the cremaster. God will never force His attachment on us. We need to want it, ask for it, and seek it. He will be faithful in His part of securing and holding us there. But we need to vow to the commitment to make the climb and attach to His holy hook.

> My choice to climb was underway.

Just like the caterpillar sheds its outer shell, I needed to strip any remnants that were no longer suiting my inner wardrobe for the promise of wings. That's what uncovering is. It's the shedding and stripping away of our falsehood, better known as our fabricated ego, releasing the unfavorable strongholds that keep us clenched. Our appealing, authentic parts already have His original stamp of approval. He keeps all that is real. And in our undressing, may we not overlook how our emotions play a role. We also need to face them with the Lord; for the weightiness within unresolved anger, unforgiving grudges, and impending jealousy leads to soul cancers of today.

> Get rid of all bitterness, rage, anger, harsh words, and slander, as well as all types of evil behavior. —Ephesians 4:31 (NIV)

> And what we often cling to the most
> may be the very thing in need of release.

> UNCOVERING is Biblical Healthiness!

Throw off *everything* that hinders and the sin that so easily entangles and let us run with perseverance the race marked out for us. —Hebrews 12:1 (NIV, emphasis mine)

> It was time to strip off my graveclothes.

> To uncloak, unmask, unveil.

> Connecting to God's reconstruction, in a secure coupling,

> anchoring myself to The Almighty!

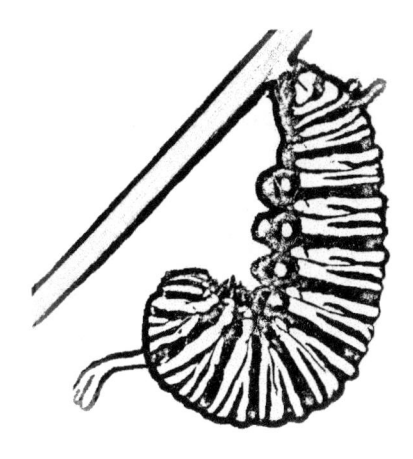

I can never have perfect rest or true happiness until I am so attached to Him that there can be no created thing between my God and me. —Julian of Norwich

Anchored in the Almighty

Before I shed my graveclothes—I needed assurance in my implanted, unshakable anchor. In the life cycle of the butterfly, this stage is the secure point where the caterpillar hangs and begins to form the shape of the letter J. This is not an arbitrary position, but a point of full surrender. Once it fastens tightly, the cremaster is in place. Its hanging formation is radical in its nature of connectiveness, marking its measure by the amount of yield. Its amazing position proclaims the promise of wings.

> True surrender is not a single action but a posture in life, yielding ourselves—our whole selves—to God.
> —Margaret Feinberg

The moment of surrender is not when life is over; it's when it begins. I was hooked into the Holy and experiencing my yielded anchor, my hinged point of spiritual promise! This union was my source of life, strength, health, and vitality. A connection no other could substitute. A connectiveness with the Ultimate and Incredible Cremaster. That place where holiness greets wholeness. It was a fastening of faithfulness that I knew from here forth could create all new things—even wings.

I love how the Lord humors. I can't help but smile heartily as I was seeing within the shaped J the first initial for His own name, Jesus. I was eager to see Him in everything, everywhere. I would often just find myself speaking His name. I was seeing Him now in spaces where I may have missed Him before, willing to waiver on the side of belief every time. For without this connective still point in my life, there would be no dance of true transformation. This connection needed to take form, first and foremost. This is where the love-covenant is established and experienced. And I was falling fast in a relationship that was going to sustain my life for all of my days.

It required dependency and my awareness of it. My neediness helped position me. He comes to fill when He knows we are empty. The utter dependence of a beggar is what beckons Him in. He knew I was living off hope alone.

> Hope doesn't promise success to the strong but resurrection to the wrecked. —Ann Voskamp

I needed some resurrected hope to remain alive. A hope in Him. Not with closed hands of fear but with open palms of faith, ready to receive. Trusting His holiness was enough to hold me up.

The Most High became my abiding place (John 15:14), abiding in a holy, sustaining center where all hope lives. The Holy Spirit dwells within the quiet core. My choice had been made. Just as the caterpillar detaches from its old larval life and clings to the cremaster, I was finding my strengthening place centered for His spin. I had found my hook-like anchor point in the Almighty One. I knew He had this and held me. Just as the caterpillar would fall to the ground if not for the cremaster post, I too knew this was my saving-grace chance to advance.

How fascinating, that the caterpillar, for a moment's time before attaching, is suspended for a split-second and is not connected to anything. Not one iota thing. Even through high-speed photography, it is recorded in that micro instant and with no real explanation as to how they do it. It's supernatural. Its suspended in midair, a freefall, fully unclenched, leaving one way of living to reach the other side. The midair suspension calls out for unshakeable trust. Is the Indwelling God asking of us the same, to freefall in our faith and trust the ungraspable mystery of His grab?

I was right on the cliff-edge, ready to fall, when God grabbed and held me. God's my strength, he's also my song, and now he's my salvation. — Psalm 118:13–14 (MSG)

Isn't that how breaking-free journeys are? That point of surrender and trust where we let go and reach up as He grabs on. That one split-second of space where only the heavenlies hold it all together. For He knows how vital the grabbing onto us is for our quest to keep going. And He then fastens us to Himself. We are tightly connected in an array of golden threads of steadfastness and love. And once the cremaster hook is embedded, it cannot be dislodged. Even after the butterfly has spun her cocoon, broken out, and taken flight, her husk remains attached to the silken pad. Christ is the vine caring for His branches (John 15:5), a lasting attachment. How reassuring to know no matter what breaks forth, our attachment to our sacred Jesus is forever placed. My branch was clinging to the Vinedresser, gaining the necessary nutrients needed to spin.

Anchored to the Almighty.

Hooked into His holiness.

Connected to the Cremaster, Christ!

Lord, I crawl to You. Anchor me under Your intimacy. Position me to encounter Your presence. Make me vulnerable to your concession. Overturn the prideful pebbles. Place me in a J shape. And do as You desire. I am anchored in You, Almighty and Everlasting Lord. Amen.

Once the cremaster barbs are safely woven into the silk pad and fully attached, then can the caterpillar toss off all the old larval skin.

I was now clothed in an unbreakable connectiveness,

savoring the secure stillness.

Both fear and faith sailed into the harbor of my mind,

but I allowed only one to drop anchor.

I had found my safe port,

positioned within the Anchored Almighty.

I was feeding on new spirit-life sap.

It was time to disrobe and deconstruct.

I knew wings were waiting for me

on the other side.

He who trims himself to suit everyone will soon whittle himself away.
—Raymond Hull

A caterpillar remains a caterpillar for the entirety of its life, or it can risk the journey to totally deconstruct and have faith that there are wings on the other side.

Worthless Wardrobe

I was diminishing future spirit wings with my own self condemnation. I was saved, sealed in the Spirit, and still wearing graveclothes. Something was terribly wrong with this picture. And my spirit was gagging from the realism. As Christians, we have every reason to be the happiest people on the planet. If we are not, we are wearing fig-leaves of fallacy. We all have graveclothes that are grossly outdated and need to be thrown. I needed to ditch my depressing duds. My wardrobe no longer flattered or suited this saved sinner. For I dressed in distressing rags of another's approval. I knew the root of my sin and from where it stemmed. I also knew His spoken words. I just didn't know how to wear His truth on an internal, cellular level. I was now growing passionate in finding my worthiness within His holy and true Word.

The fear of human opinion disables; trusting in God protects you from that. —Proverbs 29:25 (MSG)

Am I now trying to please men, I would not be a servant of Christ. —Galatians 1:10 (NIV)

The Lord Almighty is the One you are to regard as Holy. —Isaiah 8:13 (NIV)

In junior and senior high school, I began to feel an internal unhappiness. My need to appease the happening crowd was encroaching on my more authentic self. I had grown to assess my feelings based on the acceptance of others. The approval of others is a great thief of self-authenticity.

Within my inner world, fitting in seemed safer than standing out. Although my outer attire was appealing and updated, I dressed my interior spirit in all-too-familiar garments that were one-size-fits-all. It was an improper fit for me. Much like our biblical brother, shepherd boy David, who tried fitting into Saul's attire before his battle with Goliath. (1 Samuel 17:38-39 NIV); Then Saul dressed David in his own tunic. He put a coat of armor on him and a bronze helmet on his head. David fastened on his sword over the tunic and tried walking around, because he was not used to them.

"'I cannot go in these," he said to Saul, "because I am not used to them." So he took them off.

So. He. Took. Them. Off.

They authentically weren't fitting for him.

They were never David's to wear.

I too no longer could wear something that just didn't fit. We are too unique to fit into another's authenticity. The glory of God shines differently through each of us. We are not meant to cover up our shine or strength in any duplicated suit. No wonder my worthless wardrobe lacked individuality, luster, and an anointing of vibrancy. I wasn't yet wearing my own tailored fit. I was still expressionless toward my more exclusive design, a bit colorless to my more diverse character. My inner apparel lacked its own royal flare and rich distinction. I wasn't wearing my own suited shine. My fear of perceived rejection pressured me to conform closer, to a safer sameness. I was still wearing old attitudes and thought processes from the far back of my closet, miserably mismatching my true worth and unsuitable to the Worthy One.

Upon rising, I would look in the mirror and see a faulty self in need of an injection of another's approval. The affirmation and approval of others was now my drug of choice. I often dressed in a low self-esteem sweater while slipping into shoes of inferiority. I rarely left the house without my comparison coat or jealousy jacket—depending on the crowd of the day.

I wasn't then living for an audience of one nor believing in my brighter worth. The opinions, thoughts, judgments, and labels of others crammed my closet with a worthless wardrobe. I would often slip a strapped bag of bondage over my shoulder and carry around its weighty contents. I was finding myself beginning to wear dresses of depression, blackened in fearful fashions. My wardrobe was coordinated around an unworthiness that was never mine to wear, and I was wearing myself out.

Nothing was fitting or flattering. I was wearing colors of self-criticism and fibers of favorite little let-me-downs. And they were appearing distasteful against my original sanguine skin tone and personality.

But thankfully, the former patterns of my false self were beginning to feel like outgrown sweaters; way too tight for comfort. I needed something that fit the who of my original soul-self. My graveclothes of drinking from a dry well held me thirsty no longer. I was choosing custom-made clothes by the Divine Creator and beginning to wear His more legendary designer labels.

> I was readying to shed my fear of man and the insecurity that came along with it.

Colossians 3:9–11 MSG spoke its truth: "You're done with that old life. It's like a filthy set of ill-fitting clothes you've stripped off and put in the fire. Now you're dressed in a new wardrobe. Every item of your new way of life is custom-made by the Creator, with His label on it. All the old fashions are now obsolete!"

I began the great strip-down, replacing former rags for a more redeemable attire. Real warrior chicks (aka battling princesses) are found girded in Christ's love, wearing a readiness to fight off the fierce strongholds for real identity. Unlike the world's ever-changing faddish outerwear, His inner reflection is the never-changing wardrobe of electrifying attractiveness. God already has supplied our wardrobe throughout all decades, centuries, and ages of time.

We just need to PUT IT ON!

Be prepared. You're up against far more than you can handle on your own. Take all the help you can get, every weapon God has issued, so that when it's all over but the shouting you'll still be on your feet. Truth, righteousness, peace, faith, and salvation are more than words. Learn how to apply them. You'll need them throughout your life. God's Word is an *indispensable* weapon. In the same way, prayer is *essential* in this ongoing warfare. Pray hard and long. Pray for your brothers and sisters. Keep your eyes open. Keep each other's spirits up so that no one falls behind or drops out. —Ephesians 6:13–18 (MSG)

A new strength of Spirit

became the stitched fibers in my newfangled fashion.

Dressing myself daily in Ephesians Armor,

allowing His Spirit-fruit to be the adorning accessories.

Love. Joy. Peace. Patience. Kindness. Goodness. Faithfulness. Gentleness. Self-Control.

I began a complete closet sweep.

It was time to crown my head with a jeweled tiara,

in all His splendor.

Tossing everything else to the wayside that held no real value or worth,

trading in my tattered duds

for an ermine robe.

Mostly of a washed white,

sporting creditable worthiness!

Life is not a matter of creating a special name for ourselves but uncovering the name we always had.
—Richard Roh

As the caterpillar must shed its former state, so did I. Christ was peeling back the layers of mistaken beliefs, as I was clearing out my closet.

Every stripped article and inner layer brought me closer in communion with Him. I was not yet ready for wings, but I was preparing for them. I was finding my own core design and loved the truth of seeing who I was and whose I was. Every tossed rag of unworthiness brought a wave of refreshing relief. My wardrobe malfunctions were being traded in for an attire of His reflective truth. No longer did I crave the leeks and garlic of Egypt. No longer was I feeding on the chaff. I was now removing the rags of filth and making room in my closet for tiaras of trueness and an apparel of redeemed grace. He began dressing me in His spoken scriptures and His Holy presence. With a sash of salvation placed over me and a robe of righteousness draped all around, a true beauty of emerald green for His love was being bred. For had He not already paid the price for my new garments of gratitude, priceless rings of relationship, and shoes of shalom I was being asked to walk in? Its cost was the priceless, ultimate amount of His very life, immeasurably beyond what one can ever repay! Why wouldn't I respond with a responsibility to dress in a redemptive wardrobe.

So chosen by God for this new life of love, dress in the wardrobe God picked out for you; Compassion, Kindness, Humility, Quiet Strength, and Discipline. Be even-tempered, content with second place, quick to forgive an offense. Forgive as quickly and completely as the Master forgave you. And regardless of what else you put on, wear love. It's your basic, all-purpose garment. Never be without it. —Colossians 3: 9-11 (MSG)

I longed to be woven into a tapestry of His love.

So everything I touched was a touch from Him.

Hemmed within a wonder of His humility.

A more proper selection of inner apparel was surpassing my outer dress as He assisted with the soul strip. He provided paths of provision and avenues of counsel, prayer, and some holistic wellness alternative options to heal my voice. I was loving God and growing in love with my renewed self. I was desiring to spend my mornings preparing my spiritual self before my natural. I wanted to put on Christ by communicating with Him upon rising. I longed to wear the mind of Christ, the heart of Christ, the love and joy that radiates from a Christ-filled center.

I knew when the wardrobe change had taken place.

For I now wanted to Robe Another in His royalty!

I still today recall a blessed comment I received from a stranger. I was attending an outreach event, and there was a new face at my table.

After becoming acquainted, she looked at me squarely and said, "I know Who you spent time with this morning."

She was seeing some reflection of Christ within. The echo of her comment still stirs and excites me to this day. Lord, help us become more like You, displaying a lingering scent of Your victorious nature. Oh, to be a fragrance of Your presence, leaving an aroma of Your love, winging us on to express Your light. Help us in each encounter that crosses our path, to be more of You. Amen.

My inner closet was less crowded.

Creating space for the new.

I took what formerly defined me and let God define who I am instead.

Making room for the things of God,

as my wardrobe of worthiness became real.

His declaration of "No condemnation in Christ" became a seed of transformation.

Any cloth of condemnation no longer was worn.

The dross had been purged, and so had the depression that came with it!

I was draped for a new destiny.

A double destiny:

To become more like Christ

and my authentic self.

You did it! You changed wild lament into whirling dance; You ripped off my black mourning band and decked me with wildflowers. I'm about to burst with song; I can't keep quiet about you. God, my God. I can't thank you enough! —Psalm 30:11–12 (MSG)

My caterpillar legs had made the climb.

My old larval skin was shed.

I had made the choice.

And wings it was going to be!

Quiet now, or the softness of the butterfly will flee. In order to take in all of its beauty, we must be still.

We need to find God, and He cannot be found in noise and restlessness. God is the friend of silence.
—Mother Teresa

Happiness is like a butterfly which, when pursued, is always beyond our grasp, but if you will sit down quietly, it may alight upon you.
—Nathaniel Hawthorne

Chapter 4

Sacred Stillness

It was my last sighting of fluttering orange wings before winter's chill embarked on the earth. I was a bit surprised at their tardiness, for it already was the last days of November. Our yearly Thanksgiving feast, abundant gratitudes, and turkey leftovers had already been savored, marking the arrival of the year's final month. It had been an unusually warm fall in Colorado, more like an Indian summer, and this particular Monarch was in no hurry to make its migration flight to Mexico. As its wings frolicked close by, I sensed it knew it would be well cared for.

This late-flight Monarch had options, but only two. It would need to either scurry to catch up with the crisp cross winds or find a haven of safety to wait out the winter's cold. Time was of the essence. If it didn't wing itself far from the harsh elements of nature soon, it had one last life-gracing alternative. Whether through temperature extremes, possible drought, or any unfavorable environment conditions, it could be saved—rescued. God's grace was being expressed with a Plan B, through the possibility of a diapause. A diapause is much like a form of hibernation in higher animals, allowing the butterfly to circumvent the adversity of the season. And for the Monarch, its diapause can occur at any stage of its life cycle. It can occur when a caterpillar puts off the climb to attach to the plant's limb, or it can occur in the active stage, which involves their extensive flight migrations. I was pleased to see even wings have grace options. I believed this early-winter winged delight was going to be just fine. Even if it needed the refuge of a diapause to keep it protected, safe, and comfortable through the winter. It was going to survive. Hopefully, thrive.

I found myself experiencing a similar state.

My own spiritual diapause.

Freshly attached, with mourning clothes removed, I was anchored to the Almighty. My safe, sacred stillness had been found. I loved this amazing degree of connectedness. I had no desire to disengage. I knew the health of my soul needed this resting retreat. God was inviting me into His private counsel, to come and sit in stillness for a while.

My heart has heard you say, "Come and talk with me." And my heart responds, "Lord, I am coming." —Psalm 27:8 (MSG)

Quiet down before God, be prayerful before Him. —Psalm 37:7 (MSG)

In quietness and confidence is your strength. —Isaiah 30:15 (NLT)

I was placed in God's waiting room, allowing my heart to marinate in His. Prayer linked up our souls as I felt a call to "fast." Not from a forsaking of food but from distractions, white noise, busyness—just freeing myself to be and to hear.

For God speaks to those who actively listen.

Quiet down, far-flung ocean islands. Listen! Sit down and rest everyone.
Recover your strength. Gather around me. Say what's on your heart.
Together let's decide what's right. —Isaiah 41:1 (MSG)

I needed to cultivate silence, allowing space for my soul to listen. I positioned myself as a satellite receiver, waiting for His signal. Within every major event in the life of Jesus, He slipped away to be with God. How much more did I need it? I still to date, try to take one day a month and unplug from all electronics and any connection to the outside world. Just to BE. Just to be with Him. My mother taught me this.

You may be thinking, *How could one exist or survive without the outside vibe?* A total shut off from the outside noise creates space for us to hear more from Him and less from the world. The day is a gift of bringing all back to basics. I like to spend most of the day in nature (weather permitting) clearing my mind and connecting my spirit. I start with heart-worship and end with reflection. A few of my favorite spots entail hiking Dawson's Butte, Garden of the Gods, or Deer Creek Canyon. I take to the Lord my marriage, my children and their children, my health, my friendships, my current concerns, my faith walk, and the future. I wait on Him. I'm present with Him. I check in with His kingdom agenda. I thank Him for the blessings and enjoy Him within the descriptive beauty of nature. All in the shared comfort of a most casual conversation, a mental wandering from the daily doings of life. My heart finds calmness and gladness in the connection, with no need to return a text, phone, or email message—not giving my phone a single glance. I discover that fewer distractions makes me feel more connected. Maybe the important purpose of the day is letting a truer self be loved by God. Try it once for yourself. Gift yourself a day and unplug as you recharge your inner batteries. You may decide to create a "spiritual escape day" and make it a monthly ritual! The day may revolutionize your life after you hear all the Spirit Whisperer longs to share with you, for the day can have its way of revitalizing all that's real. This treasured time, intentionally set aside, IS where you meet Christ at an altar of your choice, hand everything over, and just listen to the richness of His voice.

And may we not forget that God speaks to us even as we sleep.

I will bless the Lord who guides me; even at night my heart instructs me. —Psalm 16:7 (NLT)

Let us reflect again on these words. The Lord guides me, and at night, my heart instructs me. I know God speaks to our souls at night. How often have we awoken in the middle of night to pray for someone? How often have we had more clarity about a situation or a heart issue in the first waking moments of a fresh day? In the morning's first stirrings, when our mind is not such a vigilant watchdog, giving greater probability for the deep thoughts of the Spirit, allowing our hearts to rise to the surface. Let's take our night guidance seriously. There's a reason we pray before we lay ourselves down. After a good night's sleep, there is always a clearer take on big decisions. Anytime, day or night, He waits for your stillness to show itself, for He is ever omnipresent, ever ready, ever willing to show Himself to a seeking heart. Even when our little heads are nestled tightly into our pillows and we are oblivious to any undertakings, He still speaks.

I knew the quiet was prepping my heart to hear His.

For a newness of life was arising.

I was growing to see the real purpose of the still point,

which was to *be still*

and know He is God.

How unseeing the world goes by in this age of distractions. For becoming real for His glory is not easy in a wireless world. It can get harder and harder to hear from the Intimate One in this restless, often agitated place.

And, may I add, easier to hide in a false self. The modern wall is not what it used to be. Society doesn't encourage us to be authentic. We can keep hidden and live in a false community more easily in the current day than ever before. How easy to fabricate on Facebook or send a short text, without leaving space for the real scenario in the current moment. Or not sharing how many poses it may have taken to get the perfect picture on the electronical device. We can create what we want others and ourselves to believe. Just recently, I had a beautiful friend share that she gets anxiety going on Facebook. Social media can not only make one feel like they've fallen short, it can mimic a false reality of real connection and intimacy that's not even there. In this age of independence, some find it hard to even acknowledge a need for real connection. The modern circle of connecting is changing. It's becoming an electronic connection versus a personal face-to-face one, and so much easier to fabricate and hide behind. And there is nothing more exhausting and lonesome than "image management."

Bible scholar Beth Moore spoke at a Denver *Living Proof Live* event in relation to just this. As she so poignantly stated, "We are creating a world of little narcissists." Too much self-centeredness and selfies and not enough authentic connection. Whenever we are full of self, it's a true sign of soul-emptiness. Miserable misfortunes within the reality of it all.

And through the drivenness of our modern society, most of us have no idea how spiritually tired we are inside, until we do become still. Have you ever walked into your hair or nail salon appointment with full vigor, only to find, after sitting for twenty minutes, a weariness with yawns set in? You didn't even realize how much you needed this brief retreat. There is often an unnoticed fatigue we carry as we rush around on our ant piles of life, driving ourselves like racehorses, whipping us into action, ignoring the exhausted spirit underneath. The underneath drivenness often squelches our first love. May we understand that rest is also a form of worship and sometimes the most spiritual thing we can do.

> Come unto me all who are weary, and I will give you rest. —Matthew 11:28 (NIV)

And yet, we find ourselves needing to combat the distractions that enable us to sit quietly in the intimate connection. We need to set aside uninterrupted time just to breathe. Inhaling and exhaling, drawing ourselves away and inward. His transcendent stability comes to us as we are heartfully open and available to the quiet, to the calm. He desires our drawing near, asking only one thing of us—

Not to grow impatient to be on our way.

Although we've heard the message over and again to draw near; we fail to convert. Busyness withers beingness. We've heard the acronym for the word *Busy* (Being Under Satan's Yoke), and yet we bustle. I still remember the words of wisdom imparted to me from a co-heart in Christ. She explained busyness as a heart-killer. Literally choking out the very life force within our physical, spiritual, and emotional bodies. Relationships can become timed rather than enjoyed. We can become so task-driven we miss out on appreciation, losing sight of the hidden gifts in the moments. Real gratitude for the graced twenty-four-hour time frame of life is easily lost. Just too much to do. We even overlook the profound and promised gift of each glorious day's sunrise and sunset, leaving no expression of worship to the Painter's superior strokes from His daily brush. How sadly we can race and bow down to our sacred schedules, agendas, to-do lists, and responsibilities with not enough thought of the gifts, joys, meanings, and the gold flecks of celebration that wait to be woven into the current day. I'm not trying to be completely oblivious here to our responsibilities and the many obligations our lives entail. I recognize the delicate balancing act between the doing and the being. Some seasons of life are just less manageable than others to be in this space.

But sacred stillness is holy ground.

Slowing down allows us to consider what is true and real.

Stillness promotes a Truthful Self!

It grants us the privilege to come closer, to be invited into the cloud of His glory, to nestle under His loving wings, to really see the hidden treasures found in Him.

Through a slower, more sacred holy hush.

How can we bring His presence forth if we don't sit long enough to receive it?

To be a Light-Bearer,

> we must bask in His presence
>
> long enough to absorb the light.

Stillness of soul is becoming increasingly rare in this world. Sadly, it's a bit of a lost art. Many today view "waiting" as being tuned out, instead of tuned in. Our dependency on God is seen as immaturity, versus His kingdom dependency as the prime measure of all that matures. Without silence we will lose our center. When the Spirit is stifled we lose the creative energy flow, leaving us cold and tired. We become victims of the noise instead of victors in the stillness.

> The Lord spoke to you from the heart of the fire. You heard the sound of His words but didn't see His form, there was only a voice. —
> Deuteronomy 4:2 (NLT)

Allow the silence to initiate the intimate relationship between Hearer and Listening Lord. Let it resemble that of the eastern shepherd and his sheep. Such a relationship is based on knowing the call of the One Divine Voice. Lord, raise us up to know Your voice, listen to it, and choose to follow (John 10:14,27). Seeking His voice and the fruit of it should be the #1 preoccupation of our lives. He is always speaking; His words and heart-consciousness are the source of our existence. Look at your schedule and make whatever adjustments you may need to make.

> Miss anything else,
> but do not miss the sound of His Voice.

> Find a quiet secluded place so you won't be tempted to role-play before God. Just be there as simply and honestly as you can manage. The focus will shift from you to God and you will begin to sense His grace.
> —Matthew 6:6 (MSG)

Re-robed and freshly attached to the Almighty, His works were under way. I was now only to wait on the Weaver, resting in a divine diapause. It was a time of resting. Stillness. Listening. And more stillness. I found myself in a similar neurohormonal-mediated, dynamic state of low activity. Much like the Monarch, I felt I was also preparing for transition. This space allowed me to rest and grow in God, before the entering of more. This sacred stillness first appeared as though I was shrinking away from the change instead of enlisting to enter. But I was truly allowing lasting change to take hold for the first time. My job was to seek or steal a selah and choose some self-care too. This required steering clear from the harsh elements of the winter of my soul. Newly connected, I no longer allowed abrasive thoughts, unnecessary outside distractions, or energy to go toward things that no longer resonated within. I was hanging tight with the J. Positioned. Positioned to sit and yield. Resting far from any unwelcomed rudiments that could disrupt my attachment. Opening my eyes, mind, and heart to my truest life connection, Jesus.

I was in a Selah of Stillness.

A divine diapause,

called to WAIT.

I somehow knew the sighting of this early winter Monarch would find its way home. It just had to wait a while longer. I sensed I was following close suit. For we both had found solitude, a place of replenishing comfort.

We just had to be patient.

Believing that Spring would appear again.

Wait

Poem by Russell Kelfer

Desperately, helplessly, longingly, I cried;

Quietly, patiently, lovingly, God replied.

I pled and I wept for a clue to my fate …

And the Master so gently said, "Wait."

"Wait? You say wait?" My indignant reply.

"Lord, I need answers, I need to know why!"

Is your hand shortened? Or have you not heard?

By faith I have asked, and I'm claiming your Word.

My future and all to which I relate

hangs in the balance, and you tell me to Wait?"

I'm needing a 'yes,' a go-ahead sign.

Or even a 'no,' to which I can resign.

You promised, dear Lord, that if we believe,

We need but to ask, and we shall receive.

Lord, I've been asking, and this is my cry:

I'm weary of asking! I need a reply.

Then quietly, softly, I learned of my fate,
as my Master replied again, "Wait."
So I slumped in my chair, defeated and taut,
and grumbled to God, "So, I'm waiting for what?"

He seemed then to kneel, and His eyes meet with mine …
He tenderly said, "I could give you a sign.
I could shake the heavens and darken the sun.
I could raise the dead and cause mountains to run.

I could give all you seek and pleased you would be.
You'd have what you want, but you wouldn't know Me.
You'd not know the depth of My love for each saint.
You'd not know the power that I give to the faint.

You'd not learn to see through clouds of despair;
you'd not learn to trust just by knowing I'm there.
You'd not know the joy of resting in Me
when darkness and silence are all you can see.

You'd never experience the fullness of love
when the peace of My spirit descends like a dove.
You would know that I give, and I save, for a start,
But you'd not know the depth of the beat of My heart.

The glow of My comfort late into the night,

the faith that I give when you walk without sight.

The depth that's beyond getting just what you ask

From an infinite God who makes what you have last.

You'd never know should your pain quickly flee,

what it means that My grace is sufficient for thee.

Yes, your dearest dreams overnight would come true,

but, oh, the loss, if you missed what I'm doing in you.

So, be silent, my child, and in time you will see

that the greatest of gifts is to truly know Me.

And though oft My answers seem terribly late,

My most precious answer of all is still—

"Wait."

I discovered the quiet, connective wait

was never for something.

It was about being with Someone.

An intimacy savored with the Grand Clockmaker

as He poured out His Spirit upon

my ever-waiting heart.

Moving all in its perfected time!

Are you experiencing a restless wait? Rest assured; God is at work in the wait. Waiting breeds a twining togetherness. The very word *wait* carries activity. He grew me to trust the wait, to embrace the uncertainty, to enjoy the beauty of becoming. I was learning when nothing is certain, *ANYTHING* is possible. Waiting with the Worthy One became the great gem in the journey, its brilliance unmatched by any other jewel. It's where I truly fell in love. Transformation takes time, depth, and solitude. These are the coals in the furnace that fuel the intimacy. It was the times, sitting at His feet, that brought the new level of adoration. And it only grew. Not only was I feeling the presence of His love, I was telling Him back, "I love you too." Our time together became the treasure.

> Could God be ordaining *A WAIT* simply because the delay orchestrates a deeper relationship of togetherness?

I've grown to rarely unbreak this daily space with the Expectant One. I like to meet when it's still dark outside. Letting His words sit with me in the candlelight and comfort of the fireplace, starting the day with the living Word from the Spirit of God! The predawn of the day is ours, not only for spiritual reading but for allowing myself to be read by the Word Giver Himself. It's my breath for the day, my strength for the hour, my gift of friendship for all eternity. Close friends know I'm occupied in the early morning hour. I long not to miss out on my prior engagement. It's my life-sustaining time with my sacred still point. It's really a place of expression, a place where our relationship is enriched. It draws me back to the deeper life of Christ beneath the surface of the day, to that place where I become more deeply and profoundly known and loved by God. And in return, our enmeshed relationship of love grows. He understands me like none other. He is the complete otherness.

> The great business to which I ought to attend every day is to have my soul happy in the Lord.
> —George Muller

And yet, this intimate relationship takes daily desire. We tend to be long on butterflies and short on the process of positioning, attaching, and spinning the cocoon. For these are the places where the real wings of redemption take place. The deep things of God rarely come instantaneously.

Conversion-processes are lifelong. Layer by layer, deeper and deeper, in relationship with the Upright Revealer; a little here, a bit more there, until our final remaking in God's hometown of Heaven. If the Lord had graced me with a drive-through deliverance, I never would have discovered this beautiful exchange of love or met the orphaned and truer voice of my authentic self. I cringe to think of such limitless loss. When we treat God as merely a rescuer, we miss out on the most meaningful intimate relationship of this lifetime and for all eternity.

Our connection was being solidified. I needed the waiting space of the hanging J to impede the love-trust in our relationship. I was being taught much. Even interesting new insights came through the facet of the action of surrender. I realized I couldn't choose it; it chose me. We are only responsible for our obedience, not the results. My surrendered soul was now firmed up, a bit more congealed to His, gracing me with the ability to enter into a holy dark. I knew without the solidifying of spirits, soul making would be short-lived, possibly never incubating wings.

And I was settling for nothing less than butterfly wings.

My still point was founded. Administered through the freshly woven black threads of my newly diagnosed voice disorder. I knew it was calling me to pause and reconnect with the Cremaster Christ. What I didn't yet know was how miraculous this still point position was going to be. Patty, a close girlfriend, had foreseen more than I. She knew I was positioned to spin and would come forth changed. She beheld what I was yet wanting to see. Patty's words both touched and bewildered me at the same time. As she left my patio one afternoon, I heard her speak just the thoughts I needed to hear, "I wish I could go with you. You won't come through this the same." She understood this holy place of still point I was on the brink of. Even though different circumstances challenged us to this thick place, we did share the same redemptive Savior. As we embraced in goodbye hugs, I felt the depth of understanding we shared. And I found myself tear-filled with gratitude from our shared moments together.

I was thankful for the confirmation through this woman's words. Often, all we really need is for another to understand.

> Friendship is born at that moment when one man says to another: "What! You, too? I thought that no one but myself..." —C. S. Lewis

I will not forget you! See, I engraved you on the palms of my hands. —Isaiah 49:15–16 (NIV)

We cannot make Him visible to us, but we can make ourselves visible to Him. —Abraham Herschel

The God Who Sees

Getting quiet together did grace a more connective spirit, although I am oh SO human! I now longed for a tangible, visible touch from the Soul Maker. I was experiencing a new spiritual, emotional, and mental shift, but I wasn't sensing much change on the physical side of things. The physical is always the last to get the redemptive healing memo. My voice was as troublesome to me as when it first appeared. I needed to know the Lord saw me. Really saw me. I guess He knew my need for a personalized vision message too, for His "appearance" came directly ordained for me.

It's been years since, and I still hold this visual gift in high esteem. It is an amazing memorial of His love, care, and detail over my life. I was attending an evening event in our home church and could barely speak. My voice situation had not improved, and I was losing hope for healing. I attended this outreach alone, and after listening to the uplifting voices of all during worship, I found myself downtrodden and depressed, for I couldn't even praise Him out loud. I questioned God—"Do You even see me?! Do You really know where I am? Do You really care? Why are You not healing me? What are You waiting for? What good is this doing for anyone? Have You forgotten me? Lord, have You fallen asleep? I need to know You see. I need to know You're here."

I had HAD it! I wasn't giving up on God, but I was beginning to give up on future wings.

The speaker arrived at the podium to begin the evening's agenda. I remained sitting, and wrestling with my questions before God. As I reached for a notepad from the pew in front of me, I was visually struck by His blessed care over me. There, smack dab in front of my face, was my visual that God *SEES*. I reached for the pad, and there was the most distinct penciled drawing of a butterfly with its wings spread! He was showing Himself to me in such a beautiful living expression, letting me know He never forgets or falls asleep. He was showing me that He not only sees me; He loves me. He was showing me not to give up on the wings. He showed me the wings were still ahead. I knew I had come that evening for all I needed to experience—a priceless interaction with the God Who *still sees*. I decided to leave early, for my heart reveled in the renewed belief of my SEEING God. I was filled with an impressionable joy and peace.

> "You're the God who sees me! "Yes! He saw me; and then I saw Him!"
> —Genesis 16:13 (MSG)

As I was exiting the building, I spoke a single sentence to the only other woman headed out the door. I verbally observed, "I see you are leaving early tonight too." As she replied, I could tell she had the *same* rare voice disorder that I'd been diagnosed with! Unexplainable, favorable odds. And yet, God planned our precise meeting in the foyer at the precise time. And we both knew it. We went to the coffee lounge and closed the doors down that night. I came into the evening with an angst soul and left personally touched by the Transformative One.

> My El Roi,
>
> The Living God Who Sees Me.
>
> I was thunderstruck with a Godward gaze
>
> of His Glory!
>
> God's gracious glimpse still gives me glory-bumps.

> Bravo, God, Bravo! God and all angels shout "Encore!" In awe before the glory, in awe before God's *visible power*. —Psalm 29:1–2 (MSG, emphasis mine)

No question—God sees. And His continual faithfulness *is* new every morning. It never ceases, wearies, or forgets. And we were on a roll. I now longed for my inner soul-self to be mirrored back to me through His eyes. I wanted God to carefront me honestly, expand my vision, address my shadow-sides, and show me more of Himself. I knew future freedom wings were coming. I needed to take a close look inside with the Insightful One. I needed to have my inner self mirrored back to me. I needed to revisit my past to move forward. God knew what I needed much better than I. He was leading me into another vision message, He was bringing something foreign and new, not even on my radar screen. I went willingly. I've grown to learn,

His ideas are always best.

Hymn of Promise

By Natalie Wakeley Sleeth

In the bulb there is a flower, in the seed, an apple tree;

in cocoons, a hidden promise; butterflies will soon be free!

In the cold and snow of winter there's a spring that waits to be,

unrevealed until its season, something God alone can see.

There's a song in every silence, seeking word and melody.

There's a dawn in every darkness, bringing hope to you and me.

From the past will come a future; what it holds, a mystery,

unrevealed until its season, something God alone can see.

In our end is our beginning; in our time, infinity.

In our doubt there is believing; in our life, eternity.

In our death, a resurrection; at the last, a victory.

Unrevealed until its season, *something God alone can see.*

My heart resonates with this *Hymn of Promise.*

Knowing He is the Holder of All Revelation,

things only God alone sees.

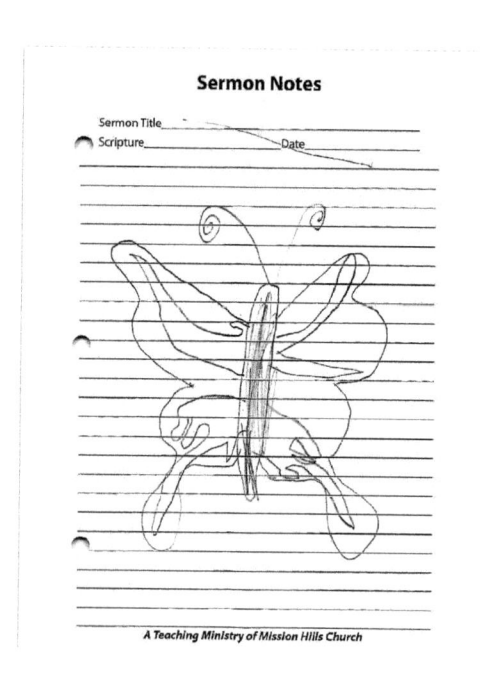

The Lord does not look at the things man looks at. Man looks at the outward appearance, but the Lord looks at the heart. —1 Samuel 16:7 (NIV)

His Reflection Mirrored Back

The Lord has "heart-ray" vision.

He is not nearsighted or farsighted.

He doesn't suffer from glaucoma

or need to wear glasses or contacts.

He doesn't see what we see.

We see dirt; He sees clay.

We see a crushed spirit; He sees new wine skin.

We see bondage; He sees liberation.

We see messiness; He sees a mission.

We see rejection; He sees redemption.

We see crippled caterpillar legs;

He sees risen wings!

I believe God honors spiritual tenacity. Just like our biblical brother Jacob in Genesis 32:26, I was willing to wrestle. He knows we can't always see the way of His workings. And I was willing to have a match with the Matchless Maker for the blessing to see myself more clearly from His viewpoint, regardless of whatever befell because of it (even if I walked away with a limp). I was grateful God didn't make me much of a wallflower in these ways. I am a God-Wrestler.

I so wanted to live out my true self. I tussled with the Lord to show me my soul through His reflective light. And through our connective solitude time, it was presented to me. An idea, a thought, an exercise of sorts. I sensed He wanted me to drop my magnifying glass, stop the internal fault findings, and

Pick up a Mirror!

I wanted to see my soul-self through His eyes. And since I've always heard the eyes are the windows to the soul, the mission assignment came. With God as my Great Optometrist, I could trust who held the power to reveal the things I had yet to see. He is capable of developing our vision. I was being asked to lay down my own introspective view with its more critical, condemning spirit and pick up His reflective mirror, to see myself the way He sees me.

So that's exactly what I did.

I found myself meeting with God for thirty days straight, looking at myself within a mirror and communing with Him. True confession. (I can hardly believe I am sharing this, but I am writing to glorify Him, and this is a beautiful piece of His tapestry and my freedom hymn.) I wrestled for the Lord to show me what I needed to see. I asked God to come and meet me. The first few times felt so ridiculously funny, almost comical. I barely made it to five minutes and found myself chuckling at the silliness.

I even got busted by my hubby one evening when he said, "What are you doing?"

I answered, with a strange comfort, "Having the Lord show me my soul."

I didn't expect him to understand, and yet in his own humble and loving way, I knew he did. I felt led to persevere. Yes, thirty minutes a day for an entire month. I drew near, never wanting to spoil the preciousness of our fellowship with visions of my own self-condemnation. The mirror reflected back to me events in my infancy and childhood. I thought about my teen years, our days as newlyweds, the births and joy of our children. I thought of my salvation day and the one who led me there. I thought about my faith journey to date. Yes, I groomed my life tapestry through the window of my soul with my Savior.

After the first week, I found myself occasionally welling up with soft tears, some from a distressed heart and others from the pure joy of seeing such a heart as His. I witnessed such unbiased, unconditional love. I remained faithful to the task. Even when we had company come for a visit or when we traveled away for an extended weekend, I made it a priority to steal away with the Soul Maker. I knew He would reward the wrestling. I was clueless of the outcome and yet wondrously enthralled with what He was revealing.

And then, around the third-week mark of this reflective activity, an epiphany came. It may seem a bit trivial, and yet I encountered such profound healing from it. I was shown the marvelous purpose behind the deepest, darkest threads in my life's tapestry. Yes, this was the epiphany; to not only know but experience this graced truth of His very presence. To know He stood alongside me in every square inch under every single enterprise! The Divine Quilter revealed how through the rigidity of my deepest desert marches, He not only drew closer still; He wove greatness. I absolutely had no inkling this was a healing need of mine, a hands-down faith-builder in my "Hall of the Holy". Both threads of my deepest pits of desperation came with such insurmountable purpose! I was shown they were the soul blessings of my life. I was feeling His love, wrapped in the undeniable truth that not an ounce of our suffering ever goes unseen by the Soul Maker. And although this world will have its fallen ways, His compassion, mercy, and love never fathers such things. I was seeing how far His love really reached, His vision showing me my worth, as we mirrored toward a more delivered me.

> But blessed are your eyes because they see, and your ears because they hear. —Matthew 13:16 (NIV)

The two most seam-bursting seasons of my life unraveled such beautiful revelation. My season of postpartum depression and my voice affliction, He worked for *GOOD*. For they purposefully brought forth the two greatest of heavenly gifts grounded to me here on earth—

Finding God.

And

Discovering myself.

What He revealed, I couldn't possibly have thought or even desired. But aren't His ways always higher, deeper, wider, and richer than ours?! He graced me with exactly what I needed, revealing to me that the blackened threads *were* what brought my irreplaceable conjoint to Christ, welcoming me into the comfort of my own skin. The two most important relationships in this earthly realm (God and self) had come through the dark. Now, both were cemented in my belief system as my greatest of light. How gloriously gracious are His ways.

EVERYTHING extends from our relationship with God and ourselves.

Knowing God results in every other kind of understanding. —Proverbs 9:10

To discover self is to discover God. When we find Christ, we find ourselves, and where I find myself, I find Him. (John 17:22–23).

Jesus makes our deepest self known. Renown author, Henri J. M. Nouwen writes: "The mystery of the spiritual life is that Jesus desires to meet us in the seclusion of our own heart, to make his love known to us there, to free us from our fears, and to make our deepest self known to us. In the privacy of our heart, therefore, we can learn not only to know Jesus but, through Jesus, ourselves as well."

The only one to teach us to find God is God Himself.

I was being shown that I no longer needed to be what others wanted or needed me to be. I tended to live out the scripts and expectations thrown my way rather than being loved for who I really was. In search of approval from the empty well of others, I had never solidified my love of God and the intimate trusting relationship with my authentic self. Giving over to the images of others only silenced my own soul-voice in the process. I had compared and compromised myself long enough. Now, through all the stitches in my tapestry, I came to encounter the blessings graced to me by the God who weaves all—the beginning, the middle, and even the end.

And yes! The growing of wings in the interim.

Through my month of mirroring with the Almighty, He showed me my vision message. I believe He needed me to see that the blackened threads were more than just a pronounced outlining of my tapestry. They were the weaves where He showed up the most mightily. And I can honestly say, I knew the perfected moment when His healing lifted up its beautiful breakthrough, for I no longer saw myself in the mirror. I saw myself through His eyes. Isn't it in our darkest distress when He comes closest to us? Beauty never comes through gladness alone. Life can become terribly challenging at times and the pathway rough, but He weaves His good through it.

> God, our God, will take care of the hidden things but the revealed things are our business. —Deuteronomy 29:29 (MSG)

He reveals for potent reasons. And I believe we are never to carry revelation as an airy, carefree afterthought but to live it out as a privileged gift; to honor His ordinances of holiness, for is that not what they are? We are to cherish the revealed things with a deep sincerity and a rich awareness of their true significance. He asks us to deeply value such worthy things. Revelation is His voice speaking today, His very voice, His divine presence. May we be found valuing the true worth of these priceless gems.

During the thirty days, I enjoyed the lovely silk fabric, but it was through the cords of rougher material where He showed me the depth of His love. Father God always fashions as He pleases. He weaves beauty from the smoldering ashes. He was so gracious to show me His determined outlining and their meanings. These darkened threads had significant direction on my tapestry life piece, for His light from my strands of gold would not shine as vividly if not for the contrast against the black threads of grief and pain. We celebrated together the revelations of what His reflection mirrored back to me. Revealing that He not only sees,

He frees!

As I fell to my knees.

He never wants our faith to ride on the apron strings of another. God doesn't copycat revelation. We are too unique. Himself too creative. Our needs are too diverse. He longs to show us His devotion and love when we are sold-out to allow the Soul Maker to spin the chrysalis as he sees fit, weaving His workmanship all throughout. We remain unfinished but His. I praise Him for the tarnished threads. I now see they brought me my greatest of soul gifts. And through tears of endless thankfulness, I raise my hands to the sky.

Lord, never let me take for granted what Your hands have brought forth,
    For isn't it enough that the Weaver's Hand brings it All?

The more we let God take us over, the more truly ourselves we become.
—C. S. Lewis

An Uncontrollable Spin

I had been readied in revelation. And just as the butterfly readies itself to attach to the cremaster, our timing to wait was over. It was time, time for the uncontrollable spin. I no longer was going to fight against what needed to transpire. And though I felt so alone, I knew it was only temporal. For while hanging in the J position, I realized "submission space" is often a destitute place. There is no room for self-sufficiency. Its corridors are too tight for more than one Blessed Controller. It's where all self-efforts give up, give way. Strength in the weakness is the paradox of the spin, leaving allotted space for the reconstruction. It's where our former wilderness mentality is turned upside down and inside out. It's where our tears become liquid prayers. It's where the sealed relationship is surrendered to just One. The beautiful thing about destitution is, it's the place where supernatural changes have an opportunity to appear and to come *alive*. It's the place where we remember God has this and always will. Destitution in the dark is designed to purge us. And it is hard stuff, but it enhances us. It's a private petition between God and self, incapable of another enrolling in the same spin. I had to trust I was strong enough to let go and enter. It was my chance to grow real wings.

I believe seasons of sacred stillness position us for our earthly purpose. Positioning us to be captured, allowing ourselves to be held hostage under the spin of sanctification. Not just a behavioral change, but changing the unnatural person to more of someone with a heart-home. He knew what was coming, and I sensed it too. A transforming touch of difference, a metamorphic shift with the Almighty. I often embraced our quiet times in the hanging J and often didn't want to leave. Other times it terrified me. Who would I become? I felt as if I were unraveling at the seams more and more as He spun. Insecurity and doubt whirled within, and yet I was graced with just enough lionheartedness to know this solitary space was creating change for the better. It was the only thing that kept me centered as He spun.

The supernatural Spirit-spin was being spawned.

It was only a brief matter of time now.

My J was evolving under absolutely no power or control of my own.

The many highway miles of the eighteen-hour trek back to Colorado from Lake Tahoe, offered hubby and I an abundance of conversational time.

I found myself asking Craig a question. "Honey, how does a caterpillar know when it's time to spin a cocoon?"

He answered simply, "It's an act of Mother Nature."

I loved his answer. In other words, it's an act outside of our control. It becomes the will of God, an act of supernatural doings.

Now connected, the Spin Maker could spin. To become undone, I needed to enter, enter a holy dark, much like the butterfly's all-encasing cocoon.

But was there such a thing as a holy dark?

I had to trust there was.

It was my only way through.

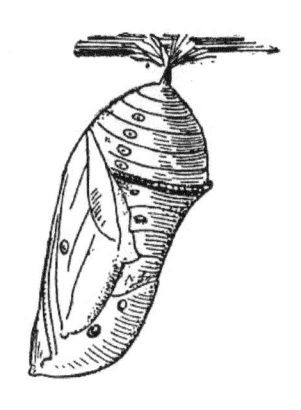

Her miracle came unannounced—and in an odd package. It looked different than she had imagined. Unpolished, Untimely, Unexpected—Unpretentious—yet it fit perfectly—divinely constructed solely for her.
—Kristen Jongen

All new life labors out of the bowel of darkness. —Ann Voskamp

For what the caterpillar calls the end, the rest of the world calls a butterfly.

Chapter 5

The Chrysalis of Christ

The Soul Maker ushered Himself in as I laid my whole in His hands. I had to go back to the place of pain and revisit its ruins to be redeemed. I prayed, "Take this heart and mind and do with it as You please." No longer was the "work" mine. This transformative place of the redemptive spin is the God-act. More supernatural than explanatory; but lasting, uprising, and real.

When God acts—who can reverse it? —Isaiah 43:13 (NIV)

What is recreated in the cocoon—in the deep—far from human eyes, is the miraculous. It's where all the soul-searching, wrestling, connecting, and revealing congeals for a rebirth. This is where the soul-making results in true transformation, rebirthing a truer, freer self under the refuge of His protective wing. Just as the cremaster is the *connective point* of surrender, the chrysalis is the *protective wing*.

Allowing a soul to be metamorphosed

in His sacred holy dark.

But never is a holy dark, really darkness. It's a space-holder for light. It's more like a protective sanctuary, keeping us away from the masses to work wholly on the task of transformation, whirling the resulted spin of His wonder. All is disguised within a sacred shroud. The miraculous weave happens hidden, far from the visible eye, the shaded environment keeps the mystery to the Soul Maker himself. Like a seed planted deep beneath desolate ground, so much transpires in the dark, before its beauty pushes above the earth's dirt to welcome the day's light.

Revealing all its glory.

And so is the wonder of the chrysalis for the butterfly's colored wings.

Its hardened outer shell is natured to protect the fragile insect inside. A secret mission is taking place in the cache of the night chrysalis, a place containing both a defense and an offense, as Christ Jesus is both our refuge and our strength. It allows an amazing rearrangement of rebirth. The first day the chrysalis is being formed is the most vulnerable stage of development in the entire butterfly life cycle. It is extremely important that it is not disturbed, for it will not survive disruption. It is now being transfigured. Real, permanent, changes are taking place. Amazing changes. I was flabbergasted to find all the changes that occur in the shaded cocoon of the butterfly. It dissolves its body and all its internal organs, rearranging millions of cells into a new structure. Its sixteen legs now become six. Its twelve eyes become two. Once it only ate plants; now it drinks juice. Before it crawled; now it will fly. Impressive changes of enormous proportion!

I stand mesmerized

as I ponder,

the immeasurable capabilities the Soul Maker has

in changing a human soul.

All happening in a holy darkness,

shielded within His Wondrous Presence.

You hide me in the shelter of Your presence. —Psalm 31:20 (NLT)

I was finding myself within the "chrysalis of Christ!" An accommodation more private than my normal surroundings, with a fragility of not wanting any outside disturbances. Oh, how pleasing it is to Him when we grant permission to rearrange our fragile. To remold—recreate—rebuild. The reshaping of His darling, keeping the loveliness while transforming the unfavorable.

A Rearranging.

An Undoing.

A Purging.

An Unsettling.

An Evolving.

Mercifully, protecting through the entire private process. All happening far from public eye, in a strategic fortress of His making. I felt a bit off-kilter again. Unbalanced. And yet I felt blanketed by the very cleft of His wing. We lived closer than before. This offered up to me a refuge to hear only one voice, strengthening me in His truth and building my belief. I found myself living in the reality of where my strength ends, His begins. I found myself abandoned within His mystery. It had been such a long wait for Him. He primed me for the sacred spin and must have been most pleasantly relieved when I finally consigned to His swirling touch.

He lifted me out of the ditch, pulled me from deep mud. He stood me up on a solid rock to make sure I wouldn't slip. He taught me how to sing the latest God-song. More and more people are seeing this: they enter the mystery, abandoning themselves to God. —Psalm 40:2-5 (MSG)

This shelled sanctuary gave me permission to return to the point of pain and self-fabrication. It called me to revisit the former ruins, to resurrect more whole, bringing the unhealed and untouched parts of myself to Him. I claimed in heart-agreement that before the creation of the world, God plans for my redemption and yours (1 Peter 1:19–20). This is a very powerful thought of belief.

Pain redeemed impresses me more than pain removed. —Philip Yancey

To get where I wanted to go, I needed to *go through*. It truly is where we want to be all along; except we busy ourselves, pushing and pulling to what we think it should be. We need to go through. We need to go through the fear before the peace, the grief before the comfort, the want before the plenty, the dark before the light. To find healing and freedom, we need to go back to where the hurt began. The going through is where the Healer and the hurt collide. This captive dark allows us to be ransomed with a redeemable restoration.

This IS the holy dark.

That place of return.

Going back to the abyss of the wound,

the chrysalis provides the Go-Through

for the Miracle to Break Forth.

To trust God in the light is nothing but trusting Him in the dark—that is faith. —C. H. Spurgeon

Never be afraid to trust an unknown future to a known God.
—Corrie ten Boom

The chrysalis of Christ is the transformation site! Letting the sadness, anger, grief, frustration, and injustice—

Run Wild.

    Run amuck.

        Run rampant.

            Run through.

                Run out.

                    Run red in His Calvary love.

There is an extraordinary understanding found in this holy dark.

There is no judgment from the Judge of Justice, only a discovery of being loved, just as you are from the Merciful Mediator. This allows an approved return to the place of the originated inflammation of anguish. As the holy spun dark, it became like a photographer's darkroom. Christ was shining His photographic visions upon me, as we waited together for them to process. My purposed picture-image came more into view. I was nourished, loved, cherished, accepted, encouraged, strengthened, and changed under this internal light. The process created a truer picture of the real me. The holy dark is one of God's greatest gifts and one of His most useful tools. It pushes, pulls, and remakes us. And yet truthfully, it is difficult and scary. I had to learn it is not something to run from; instead, I grew to understand it is God's graciousness for the betterment of my soul's growth. For when everything feels like it's falling apart,—what if it is truly falling together?

> In the depth of Winter, I finally learned that there was in me an invincible Summer. —Albert Camus

Most transformative works are accomplished in the dark. Darkness is what summons the light. In Christ's thirty-three years of life, His most significant events came out of the bowels of darkness: His birth, His arrest, His crucifixion, His death, and His resurrection from the shaded tomb. From holy darkness comes the greatest of light! Even the beginning Genesis light was fashioned out of darkness.

God already knew my new creation. For the Mighty Craftsman works heartily at His carpenter's bench. He sees the re-creation of all the endless rough edges and sandpapers the false imperfections of fabrication that need restructuring. He carves carefully, knowing how to utilize each woodchip. He rejoices in reshaping the created sweet spot in each angelic soul, whittling away until we are closer to His envisioned idea.

> I saw an angel within and carved away until I set her free.
> —Michelangelo

Christ chisels deep within the bark to free His designed sculpture inside. For what is rebirthed in the darkness becomes light. And what breaks forth from the cocoon is always more beautiful, stronger, and braver than it once was. Do you know we are often more fearful of our light than our darkness? A dear friend shared this quote by Marianne Williamson that spoke deeply to me. I hope it brings insight to you also.

"Our deepest fear is not that we are inadequate. Our deepest fear is that we are powerful beyond measure. It is our light, not our darkness, that most frightens us. We ask ourselves, "Who am I to be brilliant, gorgeous, talented, fabulous?" Actually, who are you not to be? You are a child of God. You're playing small does not serve the world. There is nothing enlightened about shrinking so that other people won't feel insecure around you. We are all meant to shine, as children do. We were born to make manifest the glory of God that is within us. It's not just in some of us; it's in everyone. And as we let our own light shine, we unconsciously give other people permission to do the same. As we are liberated from our own fear, our presence automatically liberates others."

> The worst fraud is to limit our own light.
>
> Why do we eclipse our hearts?
>
> Living under a shadow effect of a blend or suppression of self,
>
> instead of sparkling from our own radiance.

Never suppress or neglect the internal flame,

for there is nothing enlightening about shrinking back.

For who gets to say we are not a brilliant lightship of Christ?

Absolutely no one.

We can easily forgive a child who is afraid of the dark. The real tragedy of life is when men are afraid of the light. —Plato

When you come to the edge of all the light you know and are about to step into the darkness of the unknown, faith is knowing that one of two things will happen. There will be solid ground to stand on or you will be taught to fly. —Unknown

The Art of Cocooning

The cocoon appears motionless and lifeless purely to the external eye. Internally, the unearthly miracle is taking place. Even though we can't see the recreating, we trust in it as it forms, builds, and spins. Any premature exit leads directly to death. Often in life, it is in the struggle where we are made stronger. When we restrict the exertion and carefrontations, we stop the growth. An avoidance of legitimate suffering means we also stop the freedom flow. Just look at what Christ underwent on the cross, the Fierce Finisher of Our Faith. I needed to sum up a heart of a finisher to show my sincere gratitude back onto Him.

To get to where we want to go, we must go through. And God never puts us through anything He will not love us through.

A Butterfly

A man found a butterfly cocoon. One day, a small opening appeared. He sat and watched the butterfly for several hours as it struggled to force its body through the little hole. Then it seemed to stop making any progress. It appeared as if it had gotten as far as it could and could go no farther. The man decided to help the butterfly.

He took a pair of scissors and snipped the remaining bit of the cocoon. The butterfly then emerged easily. But something was strange. The butterfly had a swollen body and shriveled wings. The man continued to watch the butterfly because he expected at any moment the wings would enlarge and expand to be able to support the body, which would contract in time. Neither happened. In fact, the butterfly spent the rest of its brief life crawling around with a swollen body and deformed wings.

It was never able to fly.

The art of cocooning requires struggle. As the butterfly pushes its way through the tiny opening, the struggle is what supplies the fluid its body and wings need, further providing the power for it to beat its wings against the cocoon wall, strengthening the wings for flight.

Good timber does not grow with ease. The stronger the wind, the stronger the trees. —Thomas S. Manson

If there is no struggle, there is no progress. —Frederick Douglass

Struggle is found on the heels of all growth. If God allowed us to go through our life without any discomfort or obstacles, it would cripple us. Struggle is what strengthens our faith fibers, growing us up in every way. And if we prematurely rescue another from their cocoon of crisis, we may carelessly thwart their growth opportunity.

By wearing enabling attire.

When we permit our children to no suffering, we are doing them a huge disservice. Now, yes, there are many appropriate times we need to step in and truly be of help—supporting, comforting, and deeply caring for another. But not enablement, for when we do their work, they never develop their own muscles for managing their lives. We fracture their independence. It can be so difficult to watch a child, friend, spouse—someone we care deeply for—struggle. Maybe it's a spouse trying to succeed in the workplace, or a child grappling with a school project, or a friend or family member dazed by a painful divorce. While we instinctively will show compassion, help, and heartful care; to step in and rescue may be enabling the very process God longs to unfold within them. Our well-meant intervention may be opting them out of their very opportunity to grow. As caregivers, we often want to step in and make everything all right. We want to take a scissors and snip open the "cocoon of struggle" before its appointed time. We want to stop their pain (and often the pain we are experiencing alongside with them). But in our efforts, are we sabotaging their own ability to build the necessary inner character and strength they may need to learn and heal on their own? Are we subconsciously allowing ourselves to feel better by being the rescuer, versus truly allowing people to improve their personal situations? Are we playing their little god, believing we know what is best and acting on their part for them? May we be allowing another to carry our burden, instead of owning it ourselves? It is in the overcoming of the fears, pain, obstacles, and trials where the wings are strengthened for longer flight patterns and greater destinations.

We are a product of what we've survived!

It's scriptural.

Don't try to get out of anything prematurely. Let it do its work, so you become mature and well-developed. —James 1:4 (MSG)

Don't try to squirm out of your problems. For when your patience is finally in full bloom, then you will be ready for anything, strong in character, full and complete. —James 1:4 (LB)

I was in His holy dark. Could I make it through more than I thought I could? I had prayer questions. Would the shedding of my old embedded patterns of living truly cease? Was my more authentic self willing to break through to truly grow wings? Were the disinherited, denied, and undiscovered parts of myself finally found and ready for flight?

I was in a creative holding pattern, waiting until His effervescent light shone through my shell, waiting on the necessary work to be accomplished through my Chrysalis-Carrier Christ, who holds the weave of all transformation.

Like the planting of a celestial seed, when the seed of a surrendered soul is tilled with the Soul Maker, His plan is activated, the promise is unlocked, the light brought forth, the life released, and the miracle started. He was offering the potential to open me up, to open my life up. Was I going to struggle through the shaded shroud? I knew I couldn't afford to stay inside. I needed to pulse through my shell to the other side. Any labor pains were beyond worthy of the final prize. After all, the struggle was bringing forth new life. There was no other option. I needed to battle through the dank shelter of the chrysalis, to grow wings and fly.

Whatever God is doing IN you, He is also setting the stage to do something THROUGH you. My shell was readying herself to break open. I could tell by the more transparent light that now shone through.

I was greatly enjoying my Mother's Day gift from the kids. Each developmental stage of the gifted caterpillars seemed to be speaking to my spirit, reliving and putting some explanation to my own soul journey. As I patiently watched the caged chrysalis in our home spin and evolve, I realized again how we control absolutely nothing. All rests in the hands of the Mighty Weaver. And all is extraordinary. Even as I waited for the much-anticipated breaking out of wings, I would find myself enthralled with how the pupa continued to change, turning a bright neon-green color and then gradually fading to a beautiful, rich jade green. Only in retrospect, I realized what I was seeing was the last of color changes and the most beautiful. Little shimmering gold flecks were appearing over the chrysalis, creating the look of a sparkling jewel; exquisite transformation. Everything new wings needed was being made alive, right before my eyes. And the next morning, I awoke to see it had become totally transparent in color. I could see the coloring and printed patterns of the butterfly wings within the enwombed casing. But truly what were my odds of seeing the birth? Slim to none, I knew. For the entire event takes place within a couple of minutes, truly a matter of mere seconds.

And yet, the next day, due to the hidden blessing of being home with our sick Labrador, Lacey, I got to witness the grand finale, the opening event. It was late afternoon as I bypassed the netted cage, mundanely putting laundry away. I saw something protruding forth from the cocoon in a disparate shape, possibly the formation of a wing. Its misshaped, emergent body was bulging against the cocoon wall. The outward bulge appeared lopsided on the right side. The startling etch of the unfurling wing formation began to sway. Vibrating, quivering, strengthening itself against the cocoon's wall. I grabbed my cell phone. I wanted to video and capture its new life.

The chrysalis was opening!

Wiggling itself free from the shell,

its husk of matter to be forever left behind.

Wings were being birthed. Beautiful, bright wings.

Its wings were wet.

It needed rest

to dry them,

Before it could begin pumping its wings again,

READYING ITSELF for NEW LIFE!

I was captivated with Christ's cause, for any born-again spirit undergoes similar analogies. In Christianity, we see the butterfly as a symbol of the resurrection of Christ and saved believers. The butterfly is a living parable promise of Christ's life within us, creating the former person into the new.

Now we look inside, and what we see is that anyone united with the Messiah gets a fresh start, is created new. The old life is gone; a new life burgeons. —2 Corinthians 5:17 (MSG)

No longer was I sandwiched between the old and new woman.

Born-again spirits break forth from:

Unknowns to truth

A stripping to clothed

A distance to connection

A weakness to strength

An entanglement to woven

A wait to discovery

A search to found

A darkness to light

A death to life

All came purposely clear, as I watched this caterpillar birth wings.

Unwrap me, Lord, and let me loose.

Rebirth me back to all I was meant to be.

Just when the caterpillar thought the world was over, it became a butterfly.

Beautiful and graceful, varied and enchanting, small but approachable, butterflies lead you to the sunny side of life. And everyone deserves a little sunshine. —Jeffrey Glassberg

One cannot consent to creep when one feels an impulse to soar. —Helen Keller

Chapter 6

Growing Wings

Damp and not yet in full-winged form, the great mystery of the glorious metamorphosis had arrived. Her wings began to move, expressing life as my heart fluttered for its fragility. It was making no attempt to fly yet, sitting on the empty cusp of her cocoon, just pumping her wings. She needed to pump more body fluid through the soft veins of her crumpled new wings, helping them to fully extend, drying them more as she welcomed herself to her new life.

And then she opened her wings in royal spread!

The inside of her wing pattern and coloring even more vibrant than the outer.

And her first impulse was to do what she was created to do.

Fly.

Still in the three-foot-tall netted cage, she made her first test-flight.

Her wings were healthy.

Her wings were alive.

Her wings fit.

Her wings flew, right in front of my eyes.

I sensed a maelstrom of emotions, for out of my Mother's Day gift of six caterpillars (named by a dearest friend's grandchildren as Charlotte, Faith, Hazel, Grace, Tiny, and Catty), Grace was the one that grew the wings! I was sensing my own spiritual journey through her transformation, recollecting all the times God so lovingly blew on my soggy wings, waiting patiently on me, encouraging my flight. I celebrated the feel and sight of her newfound wings. So fresh. So alive. So real. I felt a shared joy. Everything came together in my own heart, making complete sense of my soul journey, and yet nothing seemed sensible.

It takes a bit of time for our thoughts to catch up with the miraculous.

I longed to set her free, to uncage her orange wings. As she fluttered within the net, I knew she was ready for freedom places. Her Release Day was here. And how like God to allow this day to fall on May 30th, the birthdate of our first-born son and giver of this gift.

With great anticipation, I wanted to experience her first flight in the open skies. I was grateful Cari was in our home; one never wants to celebrate such joyous moments alone. We took the net outdoors. Among the backyard foliage, with plenty oak shrub and earthly Colorado evergreens, we wanted to see the soar of her wings! Craig and I have witnessed many of God's living creatures in this exact location over the past decade. We've been visited by wild turkeys, fox, deer, coyotes, bobcats, and yes, bears. But in this moment, they paled in comparison. For these spread wings had a more spiritual relationship with myself. I had raised her. I watched her feed on the milkweed and ascend to the cremaster. I marveled at her hanging J and was mesmerized with the spinning of her chrysalis. I was enthralled with her growing emerald-jeweled chrysalis and eventually her transparent state. I saw her birth. I watched her wet wings dry. We had journeyed together visually, figuratively, and soulfully.

I lusted for her first flight.

How extravagantly must the Soul Maker crave for ours?!

> What if I fall? Oh, but darling, what if you fly?
> —Unknown

Wild and Cageless

After I unzipped the netted cage, it took her a few brief seconds to realize all of freedom awaited. She hesitated on seeking her Canaan exit, maybe not certain if this was really—real. Perhaps unsure her wings would hold up in the great expanse of the open sky, never yet experiencing the feel of wind currents. Maybe she just needed to discover her extraordinary exit was unblocked. But when she found the unzipped opening,

She flew.

She soared!

As the mighty Monarch soared above the oak brush, beyond the evergreens, bypassing the tallest rock peak, she FLEW majestically. I watched her wings in flight until the smallest of her speck could no longer be seen. And yet I had this beautiful sense she was still watching me, her wing flaps displaying her waves of gratitude and goodbyes. I watched until her wings no longer could be seen. She had survived. She was sailing. She was free to be!

I sat among the moment for the longest time. I didn't want to leave the feeling. For it was so beautiful on so many realms. God was letting me experience my Release Day too.

In this moment,

I felt a cradling of God's current around me.

Releasing me, setting me free.

I was captivated by only one thing.

His Love!

Her soaring flight encouraged me to welcome a new level of height in my own journey. Words from the Soul Maker came to my heart. "Beyond what you can think or even imagine." I can live unsafe. Letting go of the control, the misbeliefs, the unrealistic fears, the carefully placed coverings and …

LIVE RISEN!

For out of six caterpillars, ONE made it. Could that one be me? I realized all that Jesus and I had journeyed through. My own induced Egypt and the muck and mire of all the wilderness years were never in vain. He brought forth promised wings, not wings of perfection but wings I grew to love, knowing the Wondrous Weaver wove them. My tears ran. (They still run as I write, celebrating all God's good.) Freedom feels FREE!

It awakens us to …

Every doubt

Every tear

Every hurdle

Every fear

Every truth

Every grace

Every release

Every clearing

Every becoming

Every authentic inch

Of the journey.

I was beginning to celebrate the changes. And my reactions to the changes pleasantly surprised me.

For much like the phenomenon of the butterfly effect,

the changes may seem subtle

but oh how very distinct

and life-changing they truly are.

Freedom wings cause rippling effects of greater means.

> What if the truth really is that every tremor of kindness here erupts in a miracle elsewhere in the world?
> —Ann Voskamp

The Butterfly Effect

Freshly birthed wings are never purposed for just a solo flight or to keep to their own scale of self-preservation. They are made for expansion; to be imparted to the world, to ripple outward, touching the lives of others. Our wings find their greatest worthiness when flying in the path of the "butterfly effect"—affecting others.

The Butterfly Effect's philosophy is "small causes can have large effects." The term itself was coined by Edward Lorenz, for the effect derived from the metaphorical example of a tornado (exact time of formation, exact path taken) being influenced by minor perturbations, such as the flapping of butterfly wings several weeks earlier. It's amazing how a butterfly's wing flaps in Rio de Janeiro can impact the weather in Chicago, implying how little shifts can make big changes!

Now, I'm not out to debate whether this has any scientific truth (although the scientific community has now accorded this principle to the status of a law, and this principle has become a known force encompassing more than mere butterfly wings). Regardless of the scientific findings, I love the analogy it provides, for we often underestimate the influence one soul can impress on another. It can be compelling and powerful how every move we make and action we take can have its own effects on individuals, families, even cultures, all while making impressions on the own soul within.

> Just one act of yours may be all it takes to turn the tide of another person's life.

The time was present to raise up the beautifully laced wings. Metamorphosis is dramatic stuff. We find ourselves awed to Heaven while rooted on Earth. Its symbol is of endurance, transformation, and celebration. Yes. It can't help but affect every aspect of a life, starting with a song of internal gratitude, a freedom hymn.

> Blessed is God, Israel's God, always, always, always. Yes. Yes. Yes! — Psalm 41:13 (MSG)

Without change, there would be no butterflies.

The caterpillar separates from its old way of existence, enters a time of metamorphosis, and emerges to a new level of being. There are three distinct phases of the butterfly: Separation, Transformation, and Emergence. The separation is symbolic of the uncovering of sin and connecting to Christ. The transformation is the recreating of the closer state of our original, created self. And the emergence is the recovering of what was taken from us and living liberated, redeemed. Egypt, the Wilderness, and the Promised Land are comparable to interior states of the larva, cocoon, and butterfly.

This brings us to the great discovery of our own original, unique being.

We are embellished with our own giftedness and spirit strengths. It's amazing, butterflies contain the broadest visual spectrum of any known animal and can see more color than we can. They can see UV light, which humans cannot. And butterflies have a magnetic compass in their brains that gives them a sense of direction. They have another compass that uses the sun's position to keep them on course. They also use landmarks to stay on track when they drift off course in the wind. All these strengths serve them faithfully.

Lord, give us vision to see and live out our spirit strengths too.
May we not be found downplaying the treasures You have put in us.

Small shifts of freedom came, more easily, effortlessly, freely. The shifts were real. I began noticing that something as simple as a comment over my salon spa nails, being asked a questionable question, "Is anything real about you?" A former "ouch" was now answered in an honest, humble reply. "For the first time in my life, everything is." My foundation was stable, steady, not easily shaken like before. It felt irreplaceable.

Then even more profound shifts were seen. God presented an invitation to step into my own coaching practice. This was a better purposed fit. And I shifted as I witnessed clients shifting too. I no longer felt a need to say yes when everything inside of me shouted no. ("No" is a complete sentence, by the way.) I was discovering what I truly wanted to engage in and what I no longer needed to give energy toward. No longer was I being a drifter and allowing the current to pull me along farther from where I longed to be. I was giving myself permission; permission to be awkward, messy, open, and imperfect. But real. I was giving myself permission to be me. I could be different, make my own choices. I was getting whole with myself. A former self-critic was now celebrating her wings.

You know there's a shift when you no longer have ingrown eyeballitis. The focus becomes less about you and more about seeing God in others. A true sign of transformation is when sisters of sanctification become the Joy-bearers, God-reflectors, and Light-carriers in the world. These are the transformative ones, bringing His light alongside another's path. We need to take our rightful standings in honoring, valuing, and cherishing our position of holy citizenship graced under His. His beauty is in the eyes of those longing to behold Him.

Seek it. Live in it. Shine it outward.

For all to see.

And ENJOY

experiencing the rippling butterfly effects!

Over a decade past, Craig and I were celebrating our twenty-fifth wedding anniversary on the island of St. Lucia, one of our most enjoyable vacations to date. We still speak about the amazing spa day experience we encountered in the lush jungle of this exotic island. When the excursion started, we were drenched in the warmth of humid sunshine, as we stepped onto the bus taking us from the luxuriant resort grounds to a natural springs mud pool. We bathed and rubbed the mineral-rich blackened mud all over our bodies and faces. We took on the appearance of some lost uncivilized tribe. Following the mud smear, we footed through jungle terrain to a most magnificent waterfall. Women from the spa exfoliated us with their spa loofas and brushes, removing any last traces of the native mud. (I've never seen Craig look quite so happy within a community setting.) We drank coconut milk out of the shell as we walked the rainforest path in our swimsuits and flip-flops. The excursion ended with a lovely full-body massage treatment back at the resort, in hopes of bringing us back into reality. Wholly, a dream experience.

One of the spa workers was named Gabina, who asked us to call her Gabby. We became instant friends. Gabby was a gifted masseuse, and I was fortunate enough to experience her expertise firsthand. During my massage, Gabby shared her dream with me. It was to come to America. Little did I know, Craig had already met Gabby's husband, Kevin, as he was a bartender at the resort. We chuckled with disbelief as we put the pieces together.

In hindsight, the butterfly effect was well underway. Science has shown the butterfly effect engages with the first movement of any form of matter, including people. And our connection was proving to have far-reaching effects. We were thrilled to write a letter enabling Kevin and Gabby to come to Colorado for a month with their irresistible eighteen-month old daughter, Kayla. We longed to see their dream come true.

And they came! Gabby secured a job in our hometown and acquired a six-month working visa. We so enjoyed their beautiful, calm island energy and kind, gentle spirits. One of my most favorite things was listening to Gabby sing as we did the dinner dishes. Her native island voice sounded like nothing I've ever heard. It was a soothing soulfulness, a mixture of light jazz and serene spa music, with a touch of soul; nothing quite like it. My Bible study sisters and close friends helped furnish clothing, furniture, and even toys for Kayla; meeting all their needs. They eventually moved into their own apartment. I was humbled to give Gabby her first Bible and would often find it sitting open on her bed. We shared rich dialogue of God and belief. She became my special soul sister. God was weaving His impressions through our friendship.

Most people come home from international travels with island treasures, happy smiles captured on film, and favorite memories etched in their minds. We did too. Our favorite memory grew to be our most favorite of travel treasures. We came home with a *family!*

Gabby and her family left the island,

came to America

and

found Jesus.

Expressions of gratitude overflow for the rippling effect God's love has in orchestrating hearts when He so chooses.

Over time, Gabby came to realize you can take the girl out of the island but never the island out of the girl. The swaying tropical breeze of the palm trees and humid temps ended up trumping Colorado's first winter of snow angels. She was ready to return to St. Lucia. The Lord's work was done here. It was time to let its effects ripple onward. Gabby returned with the greatest gift of her lifetime. A saved, sold-out soul for Jesus. We still stay in touch. Kayla is now a teenager and sang to Miss Nancy the last time Gabby called.

Kayla's voice was as soothing to my soul
as her Momma's voice was.

I rejoice over you thinking right now about your own rippling-effect stories! There is such beauty when we see the butterfly effect touching our lives and others. The trickling effects of God's love cannot be contained. It soars upward, higher still, making shifts for all eternity. Situations of ceilingless proportions will present themselves when we make ourselves available to connect and receive. This family is a beautiful part of our lives.

Yet, it was through the amazing butterfly effect

of God's orchestration in our lives

that we even met.

Hearts are linked to hearts by God. That friend, given to you by circumstances over which you have no control, was God's own gift. — Frederic William Robertson

One kind word. One small act. One heartfelt prayer.

Toss a pebble.

Start a ripple.

While small shifts have large impacts on others, His subtle shifts of grace were impacting my own soul too. My days grew more meaningful. My soul felt feather-light. My laughter resonated with more sincerity. Real joy was being expressed. I was free to live my life—real, no longer weighted down by burdens of building, protecting, and promoting any idealized self-image. I was drinking from deeper draughts of genuineness, jugs of faithful foundedness. And I chugged. I was so thirsty to be God-alive! I often wondered, "Will I ever be?" I had been seeking sustenance from a hollow diet, trying to fill an inner cistern from a dry well rather than living poured out; never a sign of a true self. He was making a fresh start in me, shaping a Genesis beginning, bringing me back from a gray exile, putting a fresh wind in my sails.

Making me authentically His.

And I would love to reintroduce myself.

Now the Lord is the Spirit and where the Spirit of the Lord is, there is freedom. —2 Corinthians 3:17 (NIV)

Look! I'm making everything new. —Revelation 21:5 (MSG)

Reintroduction

We are risen women. Risen, redeemed women. Women of a holy altitude. Reintroductions of the Soul Maker's worth.

So, Let us RISE!

Wearing freedom wings and taking claim of our redeemed names! We are arisen from earth-bands of sloth, depression, distrust, unforgiveness, fear—all that hinders the risen life. We arise to beauty, belief, holiness, and peace—to His works inspired by love. For Jesus Christ wakes the sleeper within. He unsticks the stagnant. He breathes in the new. We are transformed in mind and spirit, broken off from the former issue of a false self. His claim of victory over us is not an impossibility but our reality.

We are free to be

in a closer God-sewn skin.

Rising Up—REDEEMED!

This must be where all the zealous passion and infectious enthusiasm stems from—

experiencing the reality of wearing one's unperfected but OWN WINGS.

Redeemed

Righteously Found

Experiencing His Spirit

Deemed for Freedom

Enthusiastically His

Energized to Encourage Another

Mercifully Kept

Extraordinary in Identity

Doing the God Story.

It's Glory Day when you meet the real you and love what God has made. It is the dawn of a new life. The old has passed—the new is here. The suit of wings fits more subconsciously, comfortably. You know the fit is precisely for you, believing fully your airborne flight is now God-breathed. This is the placement of His glory manifested in and through you.

More than anything else, God wants your authentic self. —Philp Yancey

We get to show up as we really are, in ways we haven't before. Our mind and thoughts are free to express instead of explaining away. Relationships have a new richness—more of an appreciated celebration, less of a neediness or expectation. A new confidence is now homed, no longer needing to find its worth outside of oneself. My heart-consciousness was desiring to see Christ in every single encounter, event, and plan.

It brought along a heart-peace, a groundedness, a finding of an authentic voice. The bar of my expectancy to receive had been raised. Risen women are no longer satisfied with half-measures, allowing more to become anew.

The pages in my gratitude journal were filled with a renewed spirit of freshness, aliveness. I made entries of gratitude for the light on the next step or how humbled and privileged I was with His steadfast presence as we wrote. My risen wings brought new things to my senses. My journal entries expressed the simplicity of enjoying the scampering footprints of a squirrel in the snow or the silhouette of the orange horizon against the crisp blue sky, mapping out the bravest of evergreens. Sights and smells grew more noticeable. My spirit-heart was awakened. Everything became more appreciated as my love for life and those in it—burst forth with new buds.

I no longer looked to avoid rejection, for I no longer rejected myself. It became less about me and more about the light in another. My new-winged prayers became more aches of the heart than merely words spoken. There was more empathy expressed, less disgusting human judgment. I was viewing more through grace, with an overwhelming abundance of gratitude.

> I will give you a new heart, and I will put a new spirit in you. I'll remove the stone heart from your body and replace it with a heart that's God-willed, not self-willed. —Ezekiel 36:26 (MSG)

I was energized by my new wings. They survived much and recovered great portions of the lost. I healed deep pieces of the wounded and lived from a more authentic spirit. I began making new vows. But this time not on faulty foundation. This time, my vows were placed on the identity of my Founding Freedom Father. Embracing the subtle shifts of His grace, I vowed to let Christ's identity speak louder than any other. I vowed to stand in the light I'd been given. I vowed to be true to God and myself. I vowed to accept where I was at any given juncture. I vowed to be more openly honest with myself and others. I vowed to share my journey regardless of where it may go or who it may touch. I vowed to live as His winged delight!

Each journey is beautifully unique. My journey to realness came in stages. First, it called me to choose courage and confront my coverings. Then, there was a continual process of letting go. Followed by sacred grounds of questioning and wrestling. Farther still we traveled, with bleeding prayers in the stillness. A shared holy hope in the dark chrysalis. The trembling trust in the recreate. The belief that dazzling dark brings forth light. And the wobbly new. I was celebrating what the journey had given me, what I had been taught, and Who walked with me every single step of the way.

Christ was the Celebration!

The One responsible for the freedom wings.

Deeming a holy ceremonial celebration

for the newfound

Between the King and I.

Free to Be

Free to explore His kingdom light further.

Free to experience Holy Spirit happenings.

Free to branch out of comfort zones.

Free to partake in new adventures.

Free to pray bigger prayers.

Free to love more openly.

Free to give more generously.

Free to believe with deeper conviction.

Free to worship more zealously.

Free to live in a calmer place of peace.

Free to express the true self more unbroken.

Free to celebrate the glad surprises more fully.

Free to live this one life more passionately!

Free to soar to higher heights on

new mindset mentalities of belief and truth.

> We demolish arguments and every pretension that sets itself up against the knowledge of God, and we take captive every thought to make it obedient to Christ. —2 Corinthians 10:5 (NIV)

> Watch your thoughts; they become words. Watch your words; they become actions. Watch your actions; they become habits. Watch your habits; they become character. Watch your character; it becomes your destiny. —Frank Outlaw

Feeding the Right Wolf

For liberated wings to remain on course, we must oversee our mindsets. We need to be aware of the tremendous power and influence our thought lives and self-talk has on freedom wings. Our thoughts can be greatly influenced with a positive or a negative charge. Purposefully, I have the following scripture framed in my bathroom; "For as she thinks within herself so she is" (Proverbs 23:17). I made it gender-fitting so it could personally speak to me. We all deal with battlefields of the mind from time to time. We all know when that waging war rises within, when the crazy thinking takes hold, and the battling of warring wolves begins. But freedom wings thrive when they are spoken to in tones of truthful love. Love lassoes in the negative thoughts and disarms the lies. Reminding us of all we choose to truly believe. And I wanted to align my thoughts closer to the truths of Christ's, closing my ears to the accuser. We must deal with our thought life continually, as it is the enemy's favorite playground.

An old native legend I had written down so many years ago comes back into rich recollection, helping me redirect my thoughts to a more captivating countenance of Christ-truth. I want to share this old Cherokee parable with you.

Two Wolves

An old Cherokee chief was teaching his grandson about life.

"A fight is going on inside me," he said to the boy. "It is a terrible fight, and it is between two wolves.

"One is evil—he is anger, envy, sorrow, regret, arrogance, self-pity, greed, guilt, resentment, inferiority, lies, false pride, superiority, self-doubt, and ego.

The other is good—he is joy, peace, love, hope, serenity, humility, kindness, benevolence, empathy, generosity, truth, compassion, and faith.

This same fight is going on inside of you—and inside every other person too."

The grandson thought about it for a minute and then asked his grandfather, "Which wolf wins?"

The old chief simply replied, "The one you feed."

    The power of the mind is certainly mind-boggling. For the belief behind our thoughts directs the wind currents of any wing. What we think upon becomes our inner self. Its ability can be soul poisoning or spirit blessing. We can choose to soar or stay grounded. Neuroscientists are finally catching up with ancient biblical truths and proving we can renew our minds on a cellular level. Toxic thinking wears down the brain, creating negative shutdown or poor quality of DNA codes. And our DNA is His Defining Note of Awesomeness over everyone.

> No factor is more important in people's psychological development and motivation than the value judgments they make about themselves. Every aspect of their lives is impacted by the way they see themselves.
> —Nathaniel Brander

    Even the metamorphism and complex surface of a butterfly would not be possible unless God designed its DNA. Its DNA contains more information than any computer program ever written. It amazes me how each tiny butterfly egg already contains the informed programming for all the stages, stored in its microscopically small nucleus. When a caterpillar is still developing inside its egg, it grows an imaginable disc for each adult body part.

How immeasurably *amazing* then is the DNA of His own created kind?!

And the wonderful news is, we can change the physical nature of our brain through our thought choices. We can rewire our toxic patterns of thinking. We are not victims to our biology. We have been God-graced with amazing potential for our brains to have renewable characteristics. Therefore, continually saturating our minds in His Holy Word and truths creates transforming change. Our brains can be renewed by the power of God's Spirit and biblical truth.

> Do not conform any longer to the pattern of this world but be transformed by the renewing of your mind.
> —Romans 12:2 (NIV)

For as a man thinks, so he will be.

Our emotions also play a role in programming the heart's mind. We can't control the events and circumstances of life, but we can control our reaction to them (Matthew 7:13–14; Galatians 6:7–8). Mistaken thinking can be reversed with positive thoughts and feelings of love, joy, appreciation, and gratitude. Our mind is more powerful than we give it credit for. What we think upon becomes our reality. We have been given the mind of Christ (1 Corinthians 2:16) and are made in God's image (Genesis 1:27). So may we find ourselves thinking on such things as truth, nobility, righteousness, purity, loveliness, and admirability.

Summing it all up, friends, I'd say you'll do best by filling your minds and meditating on things true, noble, reputable, authentic, compelling, gracious—the *BEST*, not the worst; the *BEAUTIFUL*, not the ugly; things to *PRAISE*, not things to curse. Put into practice what you learned from me, what you heard and saw and realized. Do that, and God, who makes everything work together, will work you into his most excellent harmonies!

—Philippians 4:8–9 (MSG, emphasis mine)

Let us remember well—

Our mindsets have the capability to DESTROY the evil wolf through starvation.

"Thought-captivation" demolishes arguments and

every pretension that sets itself up against the knowledge of God.

When the warring wolves come,

be found feeding the right one.

And we, who with unveiled faces all reflect the Lord's glory, are being transformed into his likeness with ever-increasing glory, which comes from the Lord, who is the Spirit. —2 Corinthians 3:18 (NIV)

If you are what you should be, you will set the whole world ablaze. —Catherine of Siena

CHAPTER 7

Transformed and Taking Flight

Heading into the Wind

I had to pen in my journal this extraordinary sight on September 18, 2017. It was the day the butterfly migration began, but its peak period lasted for an entire month, with a few stragglers even beyond that point. To date, I have never witnessed an infestation of so many Monarch and Painted Lady butterflies in such a saturated time and place. It was a glorious abundance. They were on their fall migration from Canada to Mexico, soaring on God-currents. The *Denver Post* credited it to a great summer season of breeding that boosted its population. This was the theory for the flood of them coming through my state. In their wild race toward the warmth,

it was our year to enjoy them.

The first day, I saw literally hundreds while driving on a ten-mile stretch of Santa Fe Drive. I thought my windshield would flatten them or my front grill would take them out. I found myself driving extra cautiously, wanting to keep their wings alive. How silly of me; they were on God-currents, remember, Nancy?! And when I stopped at a traffic light, I rolled down my window and lifted my arm toward the sky, hoping they would alight upon me, as a few fluttered only inches away from my arm. And they just kept coming for days, into the next week and then the next. On our morning walks, we found ourselves walking through clusters of twenty-five or more at a single time, stopping at bushes to get a closer look. Or while lunching in the high country, we'd choose an outdoor patio and were inundated with their wings, often flying right up to our faces. I would spend hours in the backyard, watching them frolic through. My butterfly bush in the front yard was busy! And they loved the fall mustard-colored asters and the purple lavender, which appeared to be their favorites. An endless string came throughout the day. It led me to think upon my "truth word" I had chosen at the brink of this last new year: *Intimacy*. I found myself basking in their wings while under the Wing of My Almighty. I enjoyed the intimacy of my best friend, as together we celebrated the alluring view and our You-and-I moments.

> I enjoyed nothing more on this first day than watching their wings flutter *free!*

The abundance of their wings made the nightly news for consecutive evenings, informing us of the massive number of winged delights migrating through many Midwest states (including colorful Colorado) to their destination in Zihuantanejo, Mexico. I've seen beautiful pictures of this amazing place. It's a homeland for the Monarch butterfly population every winter. They seem to find their way home right back to where they once belonged. The pictures astound me. Monarchs hang so abundantly from the tree branches, you can't see the leaves. Their wings become the leaves. So numerous and flying so close they can't help but land on you, covering you with an unbelievable superabundance of orange wings. Breathtaking stuff. It's a beauty that I aspire to see in the land of the living.

I have a milestone birthday approaching, and I've already shared with my Craiger how I would love to celebrate life. I want to savor and celebrate this place with my husband and family (get your camera ready, Nate) and experience this sacred ground of God's majestic beauty! For the butterfly has become my healing symbol, a reminder of how the Soul Maker rejuvenates and recreates anew.

Butterflies are symbols of beauty, redemption, endurance, surprise, victory, mystery, and celebration.

I desire to dance among their glory and my God's.

In Canaan, you celebrate the transformed wings. You get to live as though God is proclaiming His salvation and sanctification over you, day after day after day! A new ardent zeal arises. It is the proclamation of the new, changed life. I could no more be silent than a flower can withhold its fragrance, or the sun keep back its light. New life calls for expression, expressions of joyful realizations.

Joy abounds,

bursting out of its former shell.

A reflection of the risen life comes *alive*

as we head into the wind.

Wild and free,

without wanting to curb the impulses

of the Holy Spirit within.

Then He breathed on them and said, "Receive the Holy Spirit." —John 22:2 (NIV)

Right in front of you is the life you have forgotten, so don't back down now. —Bob Hamp

∞

Beyond the Blue Yonder

My wings brought forth a growing awareness of the third person in the mighty Trinity. I knew the Holy Spirit lived within, but had I fully received Him? Was I engaged with Him, interacting in Spirit with my Living God? New aspects of the Holy Spirit were rising up alongside my risen wings. And I didn't want to stifle either one. For every time we encounter the living Lord in our everyday life, we are to some degree renewed.

Celebratory wings give way to sight God in the unexpected, the new, and often the supernatural. May we never stop experiencing His presence and learning lessons of truth and faith from His personal touch. Some things just need to be discovered and taught outside of church walls (but, mind you, never outside of Christ's orchestration). God is bigger than the crates we try containing Him in. He can use all things to make His presence known, even within God-breathed scriptures: a donkey talked, the rocks cried out, and a snake turned into a staff!

Is He still not the same God of our Today?

Father, Son, and Holy Spirit.

The Trinity Personhood.

And the third person of the Godhead.

Living INSIDE every believing soul.

The God of all Kingdom Come has breathed His Spirit into His people! (Just chew on that unsurpassable truth for a moment longer.) Wowzers! (a homemade word; I like to use *wowzers* when no other word quite compares). So expansive is this truth, so much to grasp, and I'm so grateful we live in New Testament times, where the sacrificial Lamb has come and lives within.

But unfortunately, we can zealously pursue the things of God without really knowing Him. We can study His Word and even teach it without experiencing Him. We can major in the truths and actions of the gospel without having the heart-intimacy behind it. It happens all the time, and it is tragic, for I believe the most important gift God ever gave us is the Holy Spirit.

Risen wings love to fly on "holy highs," not wanting to be found quenching the Spirit within. I was learning to follow, no matter where His currents went. If He was on the journey, I was in. I realized the blessed abundance of wearing wings is a bit different for each of us. His touch is individualized to fit in ways that often surprise and may not be seen by all. We are much too exclusive to Him. He knows no typical case. We are all atypical. After all, we are created uniquely in His creative sight. And we all long for the mystery. May we never become bored Christians (way too boring). We never want to find ourselves thinking we have mastered the Master. Thinking we know His every move is exactly what stillborns the Holy Spirit.

Lord, let us not squander the privilege to enjoy and experience You.

Do not stifle the Holy Spirit. —1 Thessalonians 5:19 (NIV)

Unfortunately, I was tending to keep Him in a smaller, more concealed box than His bigness beheld. And it was becoming a bit too stifling for my Spirit God. I think we all can be found guilty. And how can we know? By resisting to experience. By functioning out of mindful assumptions or principles instead of by His unpredictable leading, we can lose the faith mystery in our sighted walks. The problem is, we're flooded with generous amounts of information while often starving for His true touch of revelation. May He not find us just filled with some religious smooth sales talk, having nothing to do with His living presence. We've all had

nudgings from the Lord, and when we obediently act on them, His planned purposes come alive. We see the evidence of God everywhere or nowhere. It's all in how we choose to position ourselves. When we are ready to travel beyond the parameters of pure theology and into the Spirit life of personal relationship; God will move, moving us beyond doings, works, or efforts of our own. And I've come to adoringly call them—
Holy Spirit happenings!

I'd love to share a couple quick ventures with you. A few years back, while vacuuming, I felt a prompting from the Spirit to call an acquaintance and share an encouraging word with her. Now, I hadn't talked with Evie in almost two years. The nudging remained, so I decided to act on it.

> If I acted crazy, I did it for God; if I acted overly serious, I did it for you. Christ's love has moved me to such extremes. His love has the first and last word in everything we do. —2 Corinthians 5:14 (MSG)

I turned off the vacuum and called. Evie shared with me her current struggle with cancer and said she had just escorted the hair stylist out of her home, after cutting off all her hair; leaving her head razor-bald. (Truth be told, we wouldn't go to the salon every eight weeks if we didn't care about our lovely locks; a big loss for any woman.) Through her tears and laughter, I listened to her heart. She was so grateful for the call. She said, "It was exactly what I needed."

> Not a single part of it came through my own planning or doings. Its effects were not of my own.

Another exciting Holy Spirit incident happened recently at the dentist office. Yes, the Holy Spirit is everywhere. I brought in my earbuds to listen to the comfort of my Christian music while I went through a lengthy dental procedure and shared my selected music of choice with my dental hygienist, Janet. I don't much like the sound of the drill, the tongue compressor trying to keep my flap at bay and out of the way, nor the open-mouthed x-rays. Really anything done to me in a dental chair does me little to no delight. I knew my music would be comforting. That's why this Holy Spirit happening just sparked a power charge of glory in me.

Only the Spirit God of all Capacity could get through to my dental hygienist, as all I could provide her with was a captive audience and listening ear. During this procedure, a side of my mouth was completely numbed by several Novocain shots, causing the need to suction out excess saliva, and two mold impressions were taken during this appointment too. But the Holy Spirit still chose me to be His present vessel. Janet was led to a personal relationship with Christ as she was prepping me for a crown! Yes, unbelievable. Through a limited amount of words and more head nods than usual, Janet was saved. As her tears flowed forth from her eyes, I knew her committed life to Christ right then and there was the real deal.

Not a single part of it came through my own planning or doings. Its effects were not of my own.

The pure joy of seeing the Holy Spirit move has placed me on many a holy high. I love to be awakened to His arranged contacts, seeing the Head Organizer do the planning and then to be awed to partake in the blessings when I am completely clueless I am even a prop of choice. And should we not long to live there?! The Holy Spirit is ALIVE within and among His believers. The Holy Spirit is the one who still sways a heart, inspires a vacuum cleaner to be placed on pause, brings the most unexpected strangers to become family, does heroic acts, performs miracles, and allows us to bear fruit; all while blessing us as He craves to show Himself as our greatest adventure of all.

No wonder it's a hoot,
hanging tight with the Holy Spirit!

May we not stifle the Spirit by keeping Him in concealed confinement. He is the Life. And if life isn't feeling like an abundant adventure, it may be time to do something that stretches your faith. Live in Him and share His life with others, for He longs to flow through us and from our new wings.

Freely and without restraint.

And just recently,

His Spirit fell fresh upon me again.

> May Your love for me be like the scent of the evening sea drifting in through a quiet window so I do not have to run or chase or fall … to feel You … all I have to do is breathe. —S. Kann

> And I'll stride freely through wide open spaces as I look for your truth and wisdom; then I'll tell the world what I find, speak out boldly in public, unembarrassed. I cherish your commandments—oh I love them!—relishing every fragment of your counsel.
> —Psalm 119:46–48 (MSG)

A Kingly Kindness through Ki

My spirit wings had taken flight. And I felt lured by the new adventure. God is a God of revelation. He loves to reveal Himself through nature, circumstances, scripture, people, and of course, the Holy Spirit. And when we pray for alive authentic living, why are we surprised when we receive it? Glad surprises keep faith wings alight.

> Then He breathed on them and said, "Receive the Holy Spirit." —John 22:2 (NIV)

> Holy Spirit happenings is His very breath helping our wings stay airborne for His usefulness.

It was an ordinary day of sorts, but today I was dragging with a dog-tiredness. I wasn't sporting much zeal or joy. I longed for a nap more than a notary kind of day. I had just come off a (prayerfully) solo episode of vertigo. This ordeal made the spinning teacups at Disney World seem like they stood at a standstill. Days later, I was directed to a physical therapist to rebalance my inner ear crystals (who knew?) and I was more than three-quarters back in the saddle again. But I believe my system was still playing catch up from the whole ordeal.

I had a scheduled hair appointment and thought I'd leave a bit early to shop first. When I got to the store, the feeling to enter had left me, and I went straight to the salon, hoping to get in a bit early. My body welcomed Lisa's studio couch as she finished up with her current client.

Lisa introduced me to her client, stating, "I believe you are both life coaches."

Hmmm. Maybe this was the reason for being early. I am always intrigued by other coaching concepts and the approaches other coaches take with their clients. We sparked an instant conversation. From her ranch in Colorado, Teri's modality of specialty was coming to the aid of others in crisis, transition, and transformation through horse therapy. She has found, time and again, how the empathetic nature of a horse can help individuals, couples, and groups work through related issues concerning divorce, relationships, empty nest syndrome, grief and loss, trauma recovery, and career paths too. Teri shared that clients often end up working on issues they weren't even aware they had. She herself is a brain trauma injury survivor and found her personal healing through horse therapy, which was what drew her to this line of work with such heart-passion. I enjoyed our lively conversation, and before Teri left, I accepted her most gracious invite to visit her ranch for a complimentary session and to meet the horses. I somehow sensed the Holy Spirit was in agreement. I wanted to experience her work for myself and for any future clients of mine who could also benefit from equine therapy.

Equine therapy isn't a new idea. It just was to me. I'd heard it worked well for troubled teens. But horses are massive animals, and I've never felt completely drawn to them or comfortable around them. But nevertheless, I looked forward to our scheduled time on Friday and my opportunity to experience the ranch and Teri's work.

It was an exceptional October morning. Temps were expected to reach well in the 70s as the aspens and maples danced together in the season's grand finale. I enjoyed the sighting of the small white butterflies that happily fluttered through the autumn countryside. On this day, all was aglow. It seemed the stage for a Holy Spirit happening was already set. I was filled with anticipation as I drove through the hillside to Teri's home.

Earlier that morning, I entered my quietude with a bit of extra vigor. I prayed for the presence of the Holy Spirit to show up. I wanted to be marveled by His Majesty. I tried placing no constraints or obligations on my request but earnestly invited Christ to come along for the ride. I revisited my journaled pages from that morning. I had written down, "Praying for glad surprises!" I was already anticipating something of God's greatness. I also wrote, "Let the horse be an example of Your kingship! Let me know I'm in Your royal presence. Let me see and feel Your love. Let today's experience glorify You."

After I pulled onto the ranch, Teri warmly greeted me, and we took a stroll down to the stables. There were several horses, and she introduced me to each one. I chuckled over the horse's names. One was named Burrito, and another was Salsa. I was hoping for either of the smaller horses with their Mexican flare. She said, "The horse will choose you. You never choose the horse."

Ki came forward in his stall and chose me. He was the largest of all the horses. Really? Not funny, Lord. And yet hadn't I prayed earlier that morning to be marveled by God's Majesty and to let the horse be an example of His kingship? Ki was the chosen one.

Ki was a beautiful black Missouri fox trotter with a small splotch of white on his temple; he was the most sensitive of all the horses. Finally, some common ground I could work with. I'm more than a bit sensitive myself (when it comes to my body chemistry and how it interacts with medication, we just don't mesh or mix well). I acquainted myself to Ki with a few pats, and we headed to the outdoor equestrian arena. Once in the ring, Teri asked me to walk away from Ki and call his name. The horse immediately and calmly walked over to me. I didn't realize it beforehand, but I was seeking God for specific answers in my life. I began telling Ki something I didn't even know was a heart issue. As tears began to run, I walked away from him. But what happened next reassured me that God heard my earlier prayer and delights in answering in extraordinary ways, outside of human, fenced-in faith. The Holy Spirit is so much bigger than we make Him.

As I walked away, Ki followed me and cut me off. He wanted me to stay in the moment, to stay with my tears, to stay with the truth they were bringing out, to stay with the self-acceptance piece that I had been dialoguing with the Holy Spirit about. In this moment, I realized I was being shown to accept right where I was and receive from God all the good He so abundantly graces us with. But before I could receive, I needed to accept. My job was simply to agree with grace daily (hourly, if need be).

Nuggets of acceptance opened me up to receive more of Him, more from Him, living out more of my identity within Him.

> We must lay before Him what is in us, not what ought to be in us.
> —C. S. Lewis

I stayed with the truthful tears, as Ki nuzzled his body into me and his neck over me. (I'm only five-foot two, mind you; Ki was a big boy.) It felt like Ki was taking in my pain as I expelled the tears. I knew the Lord was asking me to not only accept the current me of today, but to also open myself up to receive more. To receive more fully, receive in ways I was not yet doing, receive more directly from Him. I knew this was today's coaching lesson from the Ultimate Coach. No longer did I want to stifle what Christ was showing me. He was waiting on me this time to fully receive His love, His light, my identity.

To Simply Receive More.

Then Ki did something that is very profound for a horse and rarely experienced. With nostrils wide, he breathed on me. He didn't sniff me or snort. He opened his nostrils and breathed on me. Teri asked if Ki just breathed on me. I replied with uncertainty, but God never lets a confirmation of His will go unknown when He so chooses to reveal Himself. Ki breathed on me again, this time in view of Teri.

She told me this was what is called the breath of God. Teri herself has only experienced it once.

Did I not pray that morning for the horse to be an example of His kingship and let me see and feel His love? Nothing like experiencing the very breath of God!

To this day, the breath of God from that moment has not left me. A kingly kindness from the Giver of all Graced Things. I knew the Holy Spirit was alive, active, and in action. How gracious of our Lord to respond in our lives in tangible ways to a request of His presence. I never want to grow wings to become only comfortable with theology, overriding the personal experience of His presence.

How can we accept His truth without expecting His touch?

For are we not most our authentic selves, when we completely consent to receive the glory of God into ourselves?

We placed Ki back in his stall. I thanked Ki with a stroke to his mane and gave Teri a most gracious hug. As she and I ventured back to the house, I enjoyed hearing a clique of chickens clucking merrily in their coop; her family dogs gingerly following close beside us. I truly was embracing the ranch and all it offered. I thanked Teri one more time for the glad surprise as we both waved goodbye.

Again, I knew not a single part of this day came through my planning or doings. Its effects were not of my own.

But God wasn't quite finished with me yet. Little did I know, the Lord was going to implement a practice training test even before I left the ranch. He wanted to see if I had obtained a passing grade for the day. He humors us, you know.

I went to start my car, but it was completely dead. Not even a stirring from the engine. Nothing. Everything was dead. Teri and I tried jumper cables, but to no avail. I tried calling Craig, who was out of state on a pheasant hunting trip, and amazingly, my dragon-slaying man answered. From the wheat fields of South Dakota (and the benefits of cyber cellular service), he walked me through every probable cause. And still, my vehicle remained dead.

Then Teri's husband recommended taking the battery out of their vehicle and putting it in mine.

I quickly replied, "You don't need to do that."

Instantaneously, Teri reminded me of my morning's lesson in one word—*Receive*. We both chuckled over the testing that was already taking place through my curriculum with Ki. Of course, God was ready to implement. Was I ready to accept and willing to receive? This became the momentary question. I chose a most receptive spirit.

My battery was the culprit, and Teri's gift of hers allowed me to drive to the nearest town and get mine replaced. As I drove back to the ranch, to return Teri's borrowed battery, I found myself singing along with the car music. I was celebrating the reality of being…

Alive on wings of Spirit-truth.

What a wildly, wonderful God.

He IS the air I breathe.

Holy Spirit happenings are rarely just for us, although their interactions are grand faith-builders. A few weeks later, the *Colorado Springs Gazette* newspaper called. (Teri had notified me they may be calling.) I had an opportunity and a platform to share my experience. The reporter for the article was a Christian as I intriguingly asked before I begin to share. I shared my prayer time from that morning, before even visiting the ranch, and explained how the Trinity Personhood graced lessons and healing. She ran with the opportunity to express Christ's works in journalism to reach a wider audience. Yes. Words were written in the community paper such as Holy Spirit, Lord, and the breath of God. Crazy good, not something we see enough of. I don't know if another single soul was touched by the article, but when I sing with the church body on Sunday mornings, I praise for Holy Spirit happenings.

It's Your breath in our lungs, so we pour out our praise; we pour out our praise.

It's Your breath in our lungs, so we pour out our praise to only You.

Great are You, Lord!

I bless God every chance I get; my lungs expand with his praise. — Psalm 34:1 (MSG)

Christ Reigns! Even within the reins of a horse. I am singing, writing, and living His praise. When God chooses to show Himself, He can and will use whatever He deems.

Don't grieve God. Don't break his heart. His Holy Spirit, moving and breathing in you, is the most intimate part of your life, making you fit for himself. Don't take such a gift for granted. —Ephesians 4:30 (MSG)

My wings were alive. I was realizing the Holy Spirit never stops working His miraculous ways (and never will). And God will reveal Himself in different ways, at different times, for different reasons. He loves transforming and surprising us in the process. Did He not turn five fish and two loaves of bread into a feast to feed five thousand, with leftovers to boot? Or how about Jonah's three-day life-changing transformation, which took place in the belly of a whale? Or the burning bush that couldn't consume itself, as it called out to Moses, so he could personally communicate with God? How amazingly miraculous are His ways.

When the Resurrected Jesus surprised a gathering of disciples with His presence, they gathered around Him in joy. Christ declared their mission; "As the Father has sent me, so I am sending You." Then he breathed a startling statement, "Receive the Holy Spirit."

They must have marveled at how they got it. They didn't have to grab Him or jump through any hoops to appease. They simply had to receive. Like breath being drawn into the lungs, the Spirit was available to anyone who had the urge to inhale! There was nothing to earn but everything to gain. Receive and experience the Living Spirit God, for the Holy Spirit is alive within and among His believers. He longs to flow freely through us and from us. Letting Himself be seen and known, however He chooses.

When did we decide what size box God fit into?

It may be the perfect time to let Him OUT.

And take a deep, long breath.

As you inhale,

allow the Holy Spirit to live deeper still,

gracing you with God-ordained surprises.

Enveloping you in His inexpressible love,

exhaling His presence to a world

in need of His Love-Light!

I am bound to live up to what light I have. —Abraham Lincoln

Love is the ultimate and highest goal to which man can aspire. —Viktor E. Frankl

CHAPTER 8

Soaring within Christ's Love-Light

I can hardly believe this happened. The timing and material were too perfect, beyond my capabilities, but so not God's. And how can one write a book on authenticity and end the last chapter in a fib? Incomprehensible. So here it is. As I was sitting on our deck, working on this last chapter, a painted lady butterfly (yes, they are still migrating through) came and landed right on my manuscript! I was lovestruck by such an unfathomable loving God. I felt it was His final signature touch, and I was deeply taken by His defining mark. From the beginning of our shared story, He's used the beauty of wings to express to me the Love Lavisher in His Living Person.

Again, I ponder. Is love not the motif that runs through all? Is love not what will be lasting, long after we are gone? Is love not the journey, destination, and way leading to all things? Is love not the reason for the

Crucifixion and the Resurrected Cross? And is God not the Ultimate Love-Light of this world and the kingdom world to come?

I wondered even more. Will there be an exchange of words when I see Jesus face to face on my glory day? Not immediately, way too much to take in through one another's eyes, experiencing for the first time a degree of love in the purest of all form. But eventually, will we hear His voice?

I know we get a new name. Revelation 2:19 promises us so. Each will be given a white stone with a new name on it, known only to him who receives it. Our new name is evidence that we are believers; the name will be a stone of our authentic character. Yes, we will be given a new name with our new heart. And how incredible it will be to see the name Kingdom Christ has chosen for us! Our truest name from our Heavenly Father. (And I sincerely thank Him for my current name in this earthly realm, for biblically, *Nancy* means "grace," and my middle name, Ann, is a derivative of Nan; it also means "grace." God knew I needed double portions of grace. And oh, how I do.) But what if the first time we hear the voice of Jesus, He speaks in a question? Maybe just one! A question that sums up our all. Maybe our entire creation and purpose for being here can be answered through this single question—

Did you learn to love?

What if that is what this entire earthly dress rehearsal is all about? Finding God and expressing His love-light to all who cross our path! Becoming light-reflectors to a hungry and hurting world, graced on the wings of the Father of Lights Himself. Are we not His very gifts? Are we not extensions of His river of love-light, cascading down from the Father of Light?!

> But for right now, until that completeness, we have three things to do to lead us toward that consummation: Trust steadily in God, hope unswervingly, *love extravagantly*. And the best of the three is *love*.
> —1 Corinthians 13:13 (MSG, emphasis mine)

Love remains the highest expression of life. And nothing transforms more than love, making us think earnestly about the legacy we are currently living and what we will leave behind. Compiling both brings us to the purpose and meaning of today's dash—that period of graced time between birth and death. And to reflect on its sum, I'd like to ask you the same question asked of myself many years ago from my training life coach, Anne.

What would you like to have written on your epitaph?

My answer has never wavered through all these years from when I was first asked. Not that I don't falter on its premises (and at times terribly), but I try to keep it in the forefront of my heart:

"Nancy loved God and others well."

We each have an inner aliveness that is His glory. It's how we express Him to others. What will be written upon the heart of your eternal epitaph?

Press the pause button, still the soul, and LIVE the question with God.

Arise, shine, for your light has come, and the glory of the Lord rises upon you. —Isaiah 60:1 (NIV)

We are the risen love-lights of Christ, each carrying our own luminary glowing lamp. Garnishing us to introduce and impart His presence to others. When we immerse and saturate ourselves in Him, He rises within, gracing us with an ability to shine. His love-light is what lasts. It is all that truly goes winged on its way. Altitude wings are the God-reflectors, Love-carriers, and Torch-bearers. We once lived in darkness, but now we are the light. These are our days of awe! Let us live as children of light, pleasing the Lord with being sanctified stewards of His love expressions and vessels of His light. This one life is but a brief encounter with this world. Any good and love we can spread—share lavishly. What we do with our dash between birth and death is what we give back to the Starry Host of All Nights—Our Creator God.

Celebrate your SHINE.

Love Extravagantly.

Go Glory-light your World!

> Be someone's encourager. Be someone's cheerleader. Be someone's biggest fan. Be someone's helping hand.
>
> Give another the courage to uncover, enter the chrysalis of Christ, and fly on freedom wings.

I'd love to share my "Risen Woman of the Week" story. I love my Bible study sisters. Each are so special in His light and in her own right. Truly a precious, close, committed group, brought together under the unfurling of His wing. Gathering with them is a weekly highlight of mine.

But today I want to talk about Hillary and her love-light. Hillary is the youngest scholar in our group, twenty-six years of age, and a Down syndrome delight. She doesn't speak often, but when she does, you can almost hear a pin drop on the cushy carpet. Her words and spirit come from her inner authenticity. What she speaks comes from a real (bit unfiltered) self. She knows not differently. And she excels in living in the present moment.

As I'm closing the writings of this book, I'm lovestruck once again by the Lord's provision, this time utilizing Hillary's heart. God knows the best way to love us, choosing the lovelights of His choice. The totality of this gift will forever stick.

After class, Hillary approached me from across the room and handed me a penned drawing of an angel. (God so knows I'm a visual processor.) Hillary is a new addition to my life, and we are just sparking a newfound friendship. The drawing caused my heart to flicker as I saw Christ's flame shining with amazing illumination through Hillary's "heart work". Between the angel's wings, she had written, "No one else could fit the U-shaped space. You do it well." And to the right side of the page was written, "Underneath God's Wings."

Really, Lord?! Wrapping up a book on being authentically alive in Christ, and this is the visual I am graced with! Your love is extraordinary. You are the Risen, Radiant One! Reconfirming, refreshing me that not only am I found under Your Wing, but I thrive when I abide there. And dearly consecrating through Hillary's given words, my shaped space fits. Hillary is soaring on Christ's love-light, spreading the Great Luminary's Light. And when Hillary's bold beam hit, it lit up my entire soul.

He will cover you with his feathers, and under his wings you will find refuge; his faithfulness will be your shield and rampart. —Psalm 91:4 (NIV)

Underneath God's wings, like that of Hillary's drawn angel—I felt found.

Finally, home.

Back to where I once belonged.

There is in us an instinct ... for renewal, for a liberation of creative power ... which tells us that this change is a recovery of that which is deepest, most original, more personal in ourselves. To be born again is not to become somebody different, but to become ourselves. —Father Louis

I'm in a full circle moment. Roots to wings. A homecoming of the heart. God is the only one who can fit us into our own skin and have us feel found. Finding home is the sweet spot where Christ's love-light arises and shines on us, within us, and through us. It brings me back to a sense of realness, finding my way back to my native true likeness. A more real, freed, purposed me.

The sweetest thing in all my life has been the longing—to reach the Mountain, to find the place where all the beauty came from. Do you think it all meant nothing, all the longing? The longing for home? For indeed it now feels not like going, but like going back. —C. S. Lewis

And yet, I solemnly know there will be many other cocoons, for there are wingless places He desires for us each yet to soar. I am terribly unfinished. But gratefully, I am found.

Rebirth of newness calls for celebration, with an illimitable amount of gratitude! A grateful heart praises. I couldn't help but desire to do so with a life-enhancing, knee-bending, soul-adoring freedom hymn of personal PRAISE. With expression, aliveness, and vitality for the light, I raced to give gratitude to the Great Grace-Giver. There were ten lepers who were all healed from leprosy in the book of Luke. But only ONE returned to say THANK YOU. I am that leper. Running back, I fall facedown at His feet and weep with expressions of amazement and thankfulness! Proclaiming praise over God's unfathomable grace. I've been delivered from a walking death, knowing firsthand what He can do in a life as fragile as my own.

Bravo, God. Bravisso!

I spend the hours in grateful reflection. Because you've always stood up for me, I'm free to run and play. I hold on to you for dear life, and you hold me steady as a post. —Psalm 63:7–8 (MSG)

In his book, *The Knowledge of the Holy*, A. W. Tozer ends with a final sentence: "We are left for a season among us; let us faithfully represent Him here."

Altitude wings are never just for self.

Graced wings are never in vain.

Risen, redeemed wings are healed to pour out.

You groped your way through that murk once, but no longer. You're out in the open now. The bright light of Christ makes your way plain. So no more stumbling around. Get on with it! The good, the right, the true—these are the actions appropriate for daylight hours. Figure out what will please Christ, and then *DO IT!"*
—Ephesians 5:8–10 (MSG, emphasis mine)

We belong to the Kingdom, and we are all just walking each other home. Light-bearing wings are blessing-givers and bridge-builders. Our light shines brightest when it shines on another's plank, spreading love; calling us to be the lightships. Connecting, nourishing, and instilling more of His joy, presence, and life into others. It becomes our pivotal plank of professed truth. Living, declaring, and vowing our truest beliefs. Building a connective unity that holds us together as it places a step forward for us both. A bridge is built to cross over, to carry each other onward, forward, upward. Plank by plank, we build, enabling us to cross over and be carried back home. Although we never return to the same touchstone the same as when we left, our planks touch one another's as we sojourn on. For together, we become the bridge over the troubled waters, willing to lay ourselves down for the devotion found through Christ's love for another and for our own self.

The Bridge Builder

An old man, going a lone highway,

Came at the evening, cold and gray,

To a chasm, vast and deep and wide.

Through which was flowing a sullen tide.

The old man crossed in the twilight dim,

The sullen stream had no fears for him;

But he turned when safe on the other side

And built a bridge to span the tide.

"Old man," said a fellow pilgrim near,

"You are wasting strength with building here;

Your journey will end with the ending day,

You never again will pass this way;

You've crossed the chasm, deep and wide—

Why build you the bridge at the eventide?"

The builder lifted his old gray head;

"Good friend, in the path I have come," he said,

"There followed after me today

A youth whose feet must pass this way.

This chasm that has been naught to me

To that fair-haired youth may a pitfall be,

He, too, must cross in the twilight dim;

Good friend,

I am building the bridge for him!"

—Will Allen Dromgoole (Her life dash: 1860–1934)

> My counsel for you is simple and straightforward: Just go ahead with what you've been given. You received Christ Jesus, the Master, now *LIVE* him. You're deeply rooted in him. You're well-constructed upon him. You know your way around the faith. Now do what you've been taught. School's out; quit studying the subject and start *LIVING* it! And let your living spill over into thanksgiving. —Colossians 2:6–7 (MSG, emphasis mine)

Immediately after typing this scripture, I closed my Bible, held it to my heart, and kissed its cover. Its words are the living breath in my lungs. Its Author is the love-light of my life! Lord Jesus, fill our days with love, light, and testimony. In the love of Christ let us stand; in the power of Christ help us soar. Let instilled freedom wings touch earth for all eternity. And all Risen-Winged Women and Men together say, Amen!

Our son Nathaniel is a Beatles enthusiast. Just the other day, we heard their song "Blackbird" as part of the soundtrack to a movie Craig and I were watching. I had to ponder the beauty of the words, for they resonated accurately with the vibrations of my soul. 'Black bird singing in the dead of night. Take these broken wings and learn to fly. All your life, you were only waiting for this moment to Arise.'

I'm hearing the Voice of the Soul Maker,

speaking to me.

"Love your wings

And

Fly."

He'll be watching for your wings beloved

As you soar higher in His holiness and wholeness,

Shining brighter in His Love-light!

For we each —

Have been waiting for

THIS MOMENT ALL OUR LIVES!

Fly freely.

Acknowledgments

I asked for fervent prayers to take an honorable stand in this call and could not have succeeded without you. I want to deeply thank you dearly loved ones, who so faithfully encouraged me to write this book.

First and foremost, my beloved Craig: You are the most impactful, showing me how truly worthy I was and am to be loved. You also were the first to tell me, "You need to write a book." Sweetheart, I truly believe I may not have wings if you had not come into my life. You are my forever *greatest* gift from God. You are the salt of the earth and the cream of the crop. I love you more—still, forever, and always.

My sons, Matthew and Nathaniel: You are the apples of this mother's eye! Because my love is so rooted in you, I knew finding my wings was never an optional stance. You are the best of the best. Thank you for being the men you are. You make the wearing of wings look easy. I already know you will never settle for anything less than God's best. And that's really all I ever need to know. My love for you both is immeasurable and eternal.

My one and only graced sister, Shari: If not for you, how would I have ever sat still long enough in a chair and kept focused? You know me better than most. I'm not the most riveted tool in the shed. But you are one of my most beloved! I never could have made the trek without your pom-poms eagerly waving to me from the stands. What did I ever do to deserve your love, belief, and prayers?!

Dearest Dad: Years ago, in the month of October, you called for one single reason. To tell me to write this book. I've thought of your call so very often. It kept my fingers moving towards completion. For *You* are the fierce finisher in our family! However will I pay you back? I can't wait to give you the first copy. Because of you, I am more of me.

My sister-in-heart, Carlene: At times, you may have wanted this book written more than I did. You journeyed with me through the pages. Thank you for *living* this book's contents before it was fully written or went to print. Through real-life matters of your own heart and in real-life situations, you soared on and upward in this book's truths. It's an honorable privilege to witness your wings in flight! They are so beautiful.

My Jilly: You live your belief and prayers. It's the essence of your very spirit that attracts me and so many others to you. When we spend time together, I feel like a piece of you is already rooted in the heavenlies. More of a gift than I could have hoped for.

"Queen" Caryl: For many years, I've been humbly privileged to sit at your "feet of facilitation" and watch you pour yourself out as Christ's conduit. You watched me and witnessed as I evolved. You taught me such truths of His love. Your radiance for His Holy Word and beautiful devotion to the most Royal One, illuminates all of us in your path. One can't help but inspire to want more! You are His love-light, and I'm eternally grateful to have been touched by the oil.

"Saint" Carolyn: You were answered prayer at the perfected time. You excelled in being my computer graphic guru and you were ever present when I cringed over a computer glitch. My very weakness is your strength, and I thank God for the provision of your expertise. I value your friendship immensely.

My soon-to-be first grandchild: I may have written mostly for you, Precious One. I so pray you carry and pass on the torch of His light in your own brilliance! There is no greater prayer over your life than for you to be a strong female force who carries a fierce flame for God. You will be needed for such a time as this. I pray for your wings, even while they are still forming in the womb. Your arrival will be one of my greatest of all glory days. I am already deeply enamored with your tiny heartbeat.

My Lord Jesus Christ: There are no words. Monumental and incomprehensible Kudos to my Christ King, where ALL love resides. Only you truly know my heart's expression toward you. There is no otherness! We labored together. Your life edified and birthed all that was brought forth. Fully Yours, I forever am.

About the Author

Nancy Gardner is an international Purpose Life Coach and is passionately known as a "freedom fighter" for another's spiritual and transformational journey. Nancy and her lifelong soul-mate Craig reside in Colorado. They enjoy hiking, snowmobiling, and rafting—almost anything in the majestic Colorado Rockies. Nancy savors her morning walks, soul-connecting coffee dates, and loving others. Nancy also enjoys decorating their home and outdoor gardening, but she remains most passionate in helping others discover their own soul's God-ordained design.

Nancy enthusiastically looks forward to hearing from you.
nancy@authenticallyalivebook.com

Lift Her With Butterflies

Bronze sculpture artist, Angela Mia De La Vega

This is a most cherished bronze sculpture in our home. It captures the full of my journey. I've had the privilege of befriending the artist and her inner beauty shines as bright as her outward work displays. I'd like to share in Angela Mia De La Vega's own words, as to what inspired her to sculpt this piece:

"I woke up in the middle of the night at the sound of my own voice exclaiming, Lift her with butterflies! I felt such giddiness inside, an alacrity that prevented me from falling back asleep. Upon waking in the morning, I saw her clearly—a little girl being lifted to the sky by a towering swirl of butterflies. With this inspired vision as my model, the sculpture rapidly took form in my studio, eight kinds of butterflies coming together from around the world to lift her to new heights of freedom and delight."

—*Angela Mia De La Vega*

CPSIA information can be obtained
at www.ICGtesting.com
Printed in the USA
BVHW03*1429120918
R9070600001B/R90706PG527207BVX1B/1/P